Play with ART templates

Trace or copy these **templates** onto thick paper and cut them out.

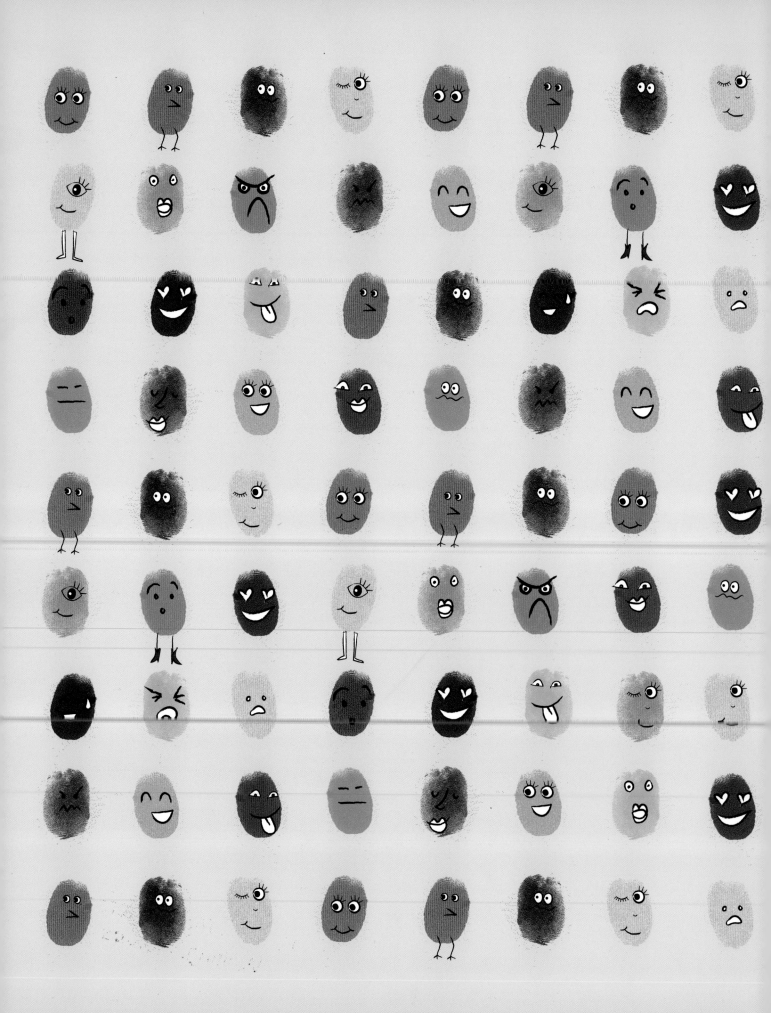

Play with ART

For the grown-ups:

This book is full of hands-on art ideas to help children explore their creativity as they experiment with different materials. For each creative media section, there is a handy "tools needed" catalogue and 6+ projects to try. Just lay out one set of materials at a time, then your child is ready to go—and parents only need to clean up once!

Safety

Children should be supervised at all times when doing these projects. They may need help with some of the trickier activities such as cutting cardboard. Always make sure your child uses nontoxic paints and materials.

Mess alert!

Some of the projects will make a mess (that's part of the fun)! Protect the area where your child is creating—or even encourage them to do the projects outside. Wearing old clothes or an apron is advisable

We made this book:

Violet Peto

Rachael Parfitt Hunt

Rachael Hare

Lol Johnson

DK | Penguin Random House

Editor Violet Peto
Senior Designer and Illustrator Rachael Parfitt Hunt
Designer and Illustrator Rachael Hare
US Senior Editor Shannon Beatty
US Editor Jane Perlmutter
Photographer Lol Johnson
Additional Photography Dave King
Design Assistance Eleanor Bates, Charlotte Milner
Jacket Designer Rachael Parfitt Hunt
Jacket Coordinator Francesca Young
Producer, Pre-production Rebecca Fallowfield
Producer John Casey
Managing Editor Penny Smith
Managing Art Editor Mabel Chan
Publisher Mary Ling
Art Director Jane Bull

First American Edition, 2018
Published in the United States by DK Publishing
345 Hudson Street, New York, New York 10014

A big thank you to all the models—Edie Arnold, Oscar Arnold, Archer Brandon, Betty Johnson, and Lola Johnson

A WORLD OF IDEAS:
SEE ALL THERE IS TO KNOW

www.dk.com

Contents

Painting and printing

Experiment with **paint** to create different **effects.**
Here's what you need:

Paper

Roller

Roller tray

What should we paint?

Funnel

Canvas (or thick paper)

Masking tape

Printing inks

Glue

Clear zip-up plastic bag

Nontoxic paint

Felt-tip pen

Pencils

Paintbrushes

Cardboard tubes

Balloons

Balloon pump

Your FEET!

Bubble wrap

Wooden blocks

String

Sponge

Flowers

Top tip
Your hands and feet are great printing tools!

Fruit and veggies

Clothespin

Paint blob

Paper plates

Your HANDS!

Your FINGERS!

What colors should we choose?

Washable plastic toys

9

Mix the colors up!

Do you know how to make **new colors?**

Primary colors

RED  YELLOW  BLUE

You can **make** new colors by mixing the three main **primary** colors.

Try these mixtures:

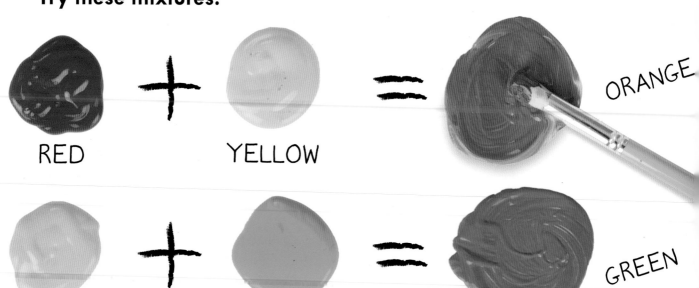

RED $+$ YELLOW $=$ ORANGE

YELLOW $+$ BLUE $=$ GREEN

BLUE $+$ RED $=$ PURPLE

10

Make your own **color** wheel

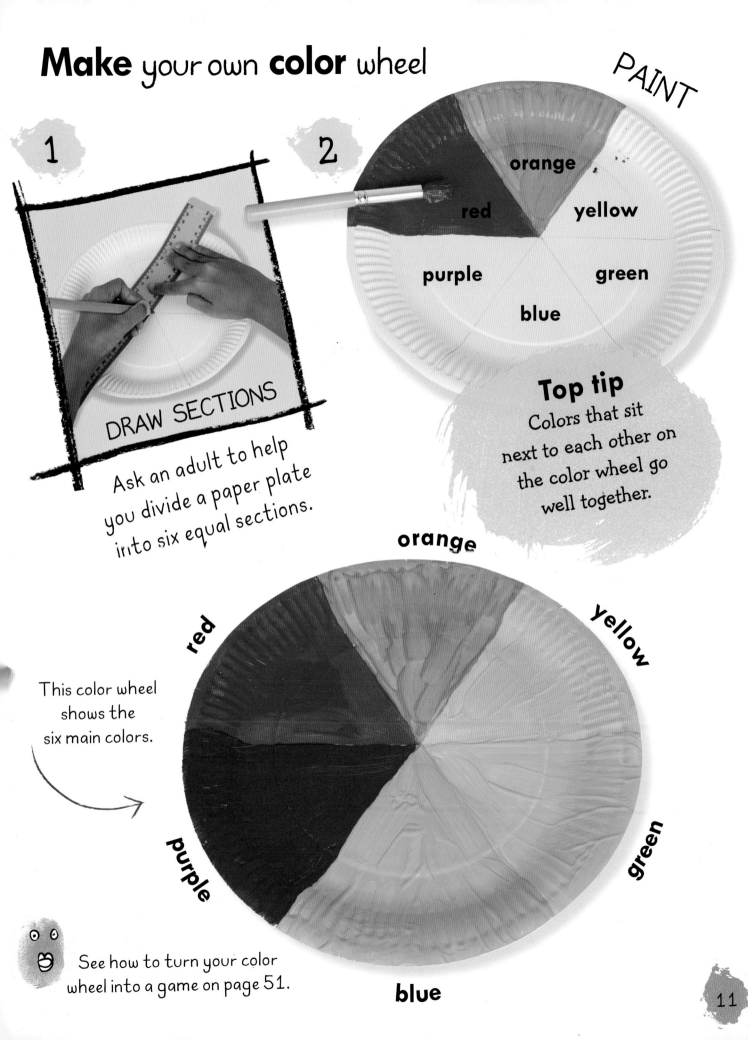

1

DRAW SECTIONS

Ask an adult to help you divide a paper plate into six equal sections.

2

orange
red   yellow
purple   green
blue

Top tip
Colors that sit next to each other on the color wheel go well together.

orange

red   yellow

This color wheel shows the six main colors.

purple   green

See how to turn your color wheel into a game on page 51.

blue

11

Printing gallery

Create lots of paint **marks** using different printing **tools**.
Here are some ideas:

Bubble Wrap feet

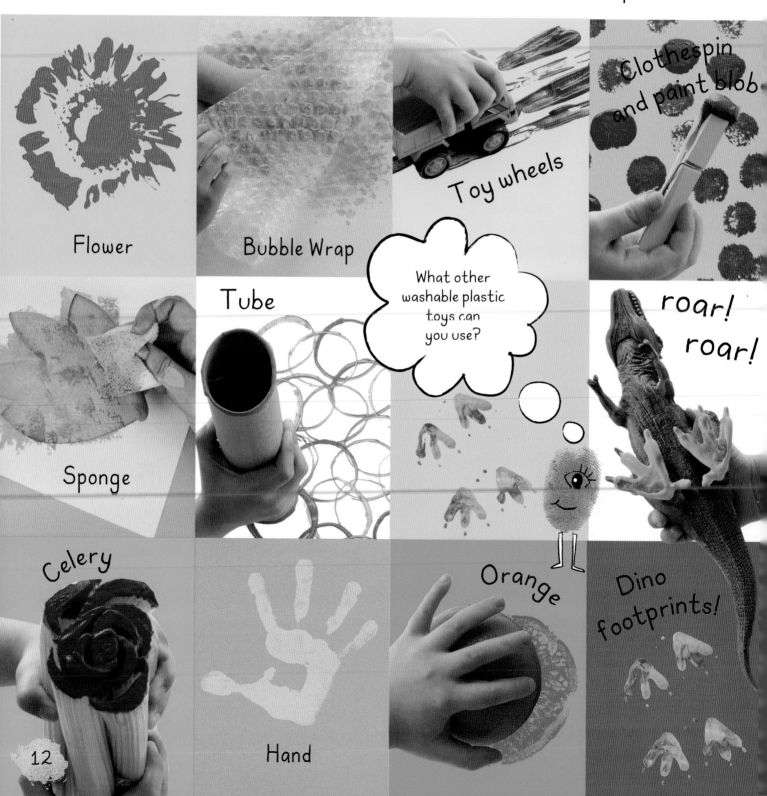

Flower

Bubble Wrap

Toy wheels

Clothespin and paint blob

Sponge

Tube

What other washable plastic toys can you use?

roar! roar!

Celery

Hand

Orange

Dino footprints!

Make your own **printing** blocks!

Tools needed:

Wood blocks

Foam or thick card-stock shapes

String

You can find heart and star templates at the back of the book.

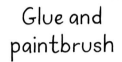

Glue and paintbrush

Roller and paints

1

GLUE

Glue your foam shapes onto wood blocks.

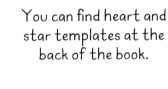

2

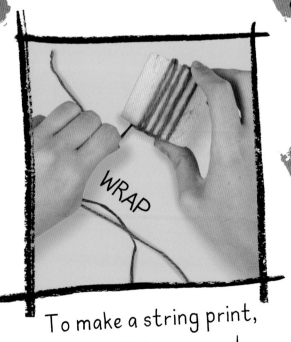

WRAP

To make a string print, wrap string around a wood block.

3

ROLL

Using a roller, roll paint over your printing blocks.

4

PRESS

PRINT

Print different patterns and shapes to make wrapping paper or cards.

Fruit and veggie fun

Use **fruit** and **veggies** to make amazing **art.**

Tools needed:

Nontoxic
paint

Paper

Fruits and vegetables

Pencil

Paintbrush

1

PAINT

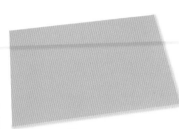

Top tip
Print a cool poster to
hang on the wall.

Cut the fruit or veggies in
half and paint the flat side.

2

FUN shapes

PRESS

Start printing! Make lots of great, colorful patterns.

Use a pencil to give me eyes and a mouth.

PRETTY patterns

Block buddies

Make colorful people by painting with **wood blocks** and **potatoes.**

Tools needed:

Paper and colored pencils

Halved potato

Wood blocks

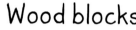

Paintbrush

Use other sides of the block for different colors.

1

PRESS

Paint the side of a block. Press down onto paper for the bodies.

Why not use blocks to give me arms and legs, too?

2

PUSH

DOWN

Use a halved potato to make the head shapes. When dry, draw funny faces on.

Top tip
Use different sized potatoes for big and small heads.

Fingerprinting
gallery

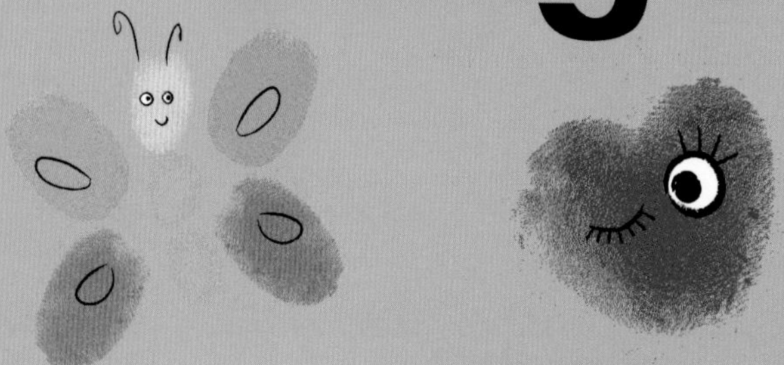

You can use your **fingers** and **ink** to make many wonderful pictures.

Use a pen to give us funny faces.

Tools needed:

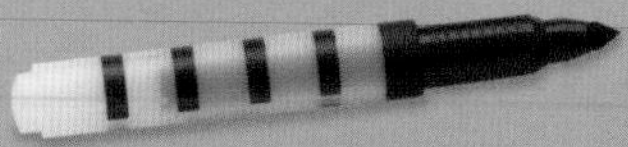

Paper

Fingers

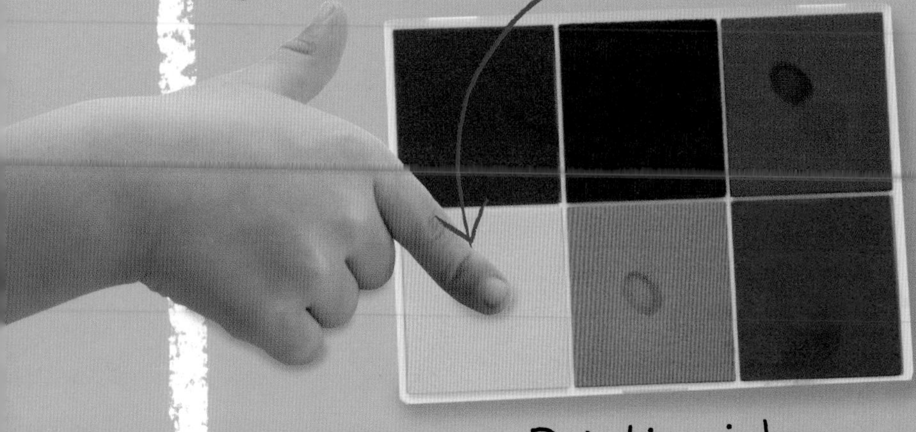

Felt-tip pen

Mess alert!

Printing inks

Press your finger on the ink pad, and then onto paper.
Use a pen to make the prints come to life.

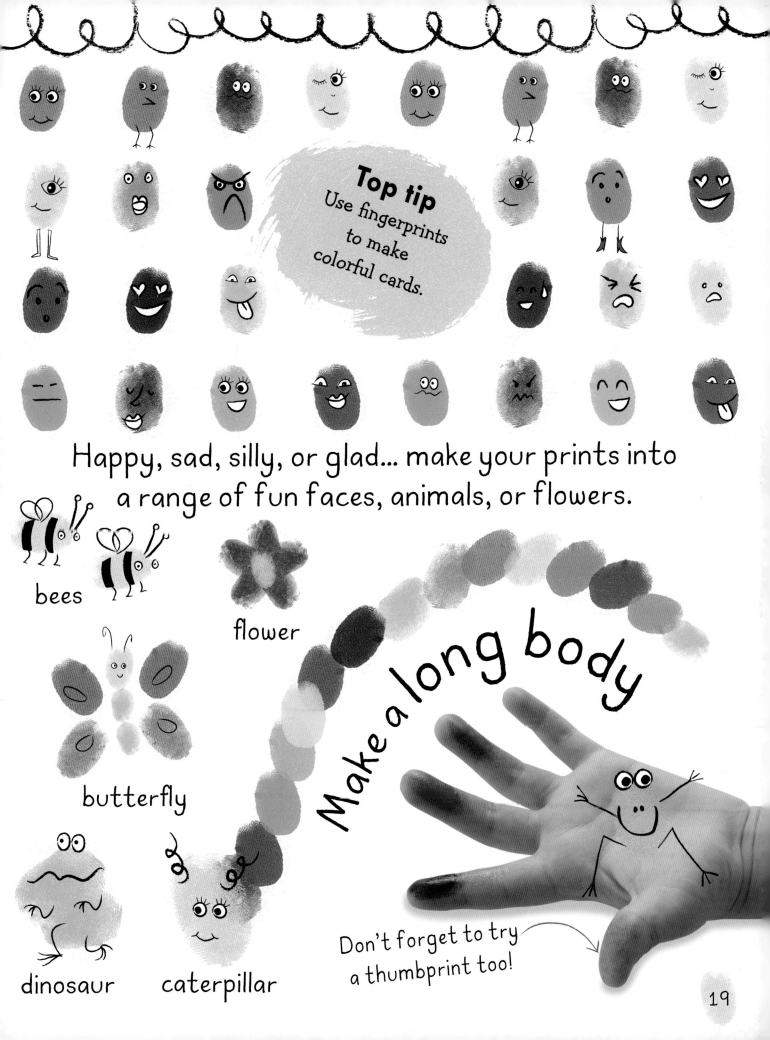

Happy, sad, silly, or glad... make your prints into a range of fun faces, animals, or flowers.

bees

flower

butterfly

Make a long body

dinosaur

caterpillar

Don't forget to try a thumbprint too!

19

Hello! I'm made out of lots of handprints.

Hedgehog

Fish

Use your **hands** to make **funny** animals!

What animals can you create? Let your imagination run wild!

Handy hands!

Mess alert!

Paint your hands and press them onto paper.

Once the prints are dry, use a pencil to draw on eyes and other features.

Flamingo

Chicken and chick

Handy hint
Make your picture into a whole zoo of handprint animals!

I have hands for feet!

Elephant

Funny feet!

Make mess-free **clean-feet** art using paint inside a bag.

Tools needed:

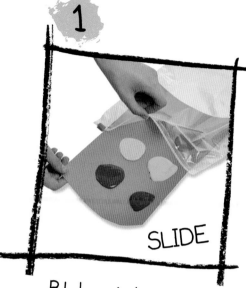

Paints

Clear zip-up plastic bag

Paper

1

SLIDE

Blob paint onto your paper. Carefully slide the paper into the bag.

Dip your feet in **paint** and make **messy-feet** footprint art! Use a pencil to turn the footprints into pictures.

Mess alert!

Bee

Flip-flops

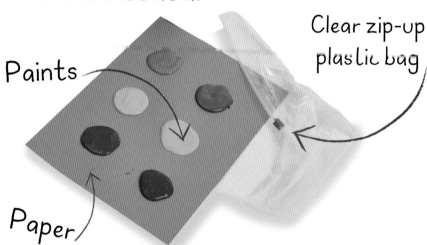

Feel the paint **squelch** between your toes!

STOMP!

Unicorn

22

2

Squeeze out the air and zip up the bag.

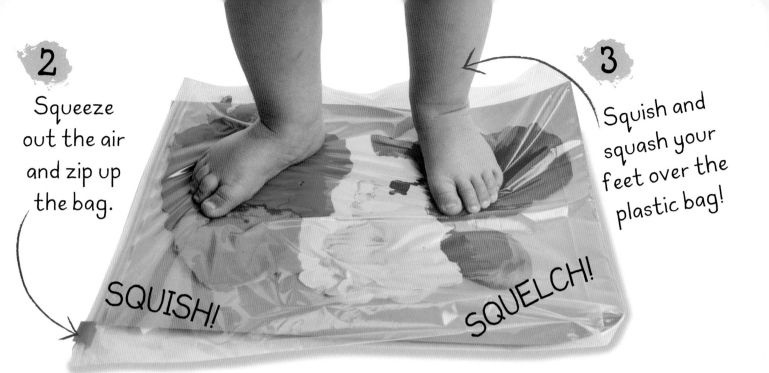

SQUISH!

SQUELCH!

3

Squish and squash your feet over the plastic bag!

Now take out the piece of paper and look at your masterpiece.

hoot!

hoot!

Owl

Cat

Lion

grrrl

Bear

Butterfly

Lizard

Try a striped print.

23

Pop! Art

Splatter your canvas and make some seriously splashy art!

Tools needed:

Balloons

Balloon pump

Funnel

Nontoxic paint

Mess alert!

This activity is MESSY, so it's best to do it outside!

Canvas (or thick paper)

1
FILL IT UP

Put the funnel into a balloon and pour paint in. Fill up about half the balloon.

2
PUMP IT UP

Take the funnel out and wipe away any paint from the balloon before pumping it up. Ask an adult to help you.

24

3

Fill more balloons with other colors.

STICK IT DOWN

Tie the balloon, then stick it onto your canvas or paper with tape.

4

POP!

With adult help, POP the taped-down balloons using a pencil.

Top tip
Try pouring two colors into one balloon.

SPLAT!

Remove the tape and deflated balloons.

SPLOSH!

Masking out

This is when you **stick down** tape or shapes and paint **over** and **around** them.

Tools needed:

Top tip
Try masking out with the shapes you cut out in the activity on page 36.

Canvas
(or thick paper)

Paints

Masking tape

Paintbrush

1 Stick down crisscrossing lines of masking tape on your canvas.

2 Paint your canvas. Don't worry if you paint on top of the tape.

3 When the paint is dry, peel away the tape to reveal a picture of lines and shapes.

Puper cruft

Find out some of the **creative** things you can do with paper.
Here are the tools you'll need:

Paper: you can cut it, fold it, wet it, shine light through it...

Paper and card stock

Tissue and crepe paper

Water spray bottle

Pipe cleaners

Ruler

Wood clothespin

Masking tape

 Googly eyes

Ribbons

Pencils

You also need a flashlight!

Glue

Felt-tip pen

Glue stick

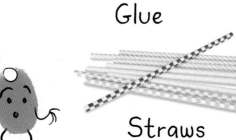 Straws

 Safety scissors

Paper folding

Transform paper into **3-D** shapes with folds and curls.

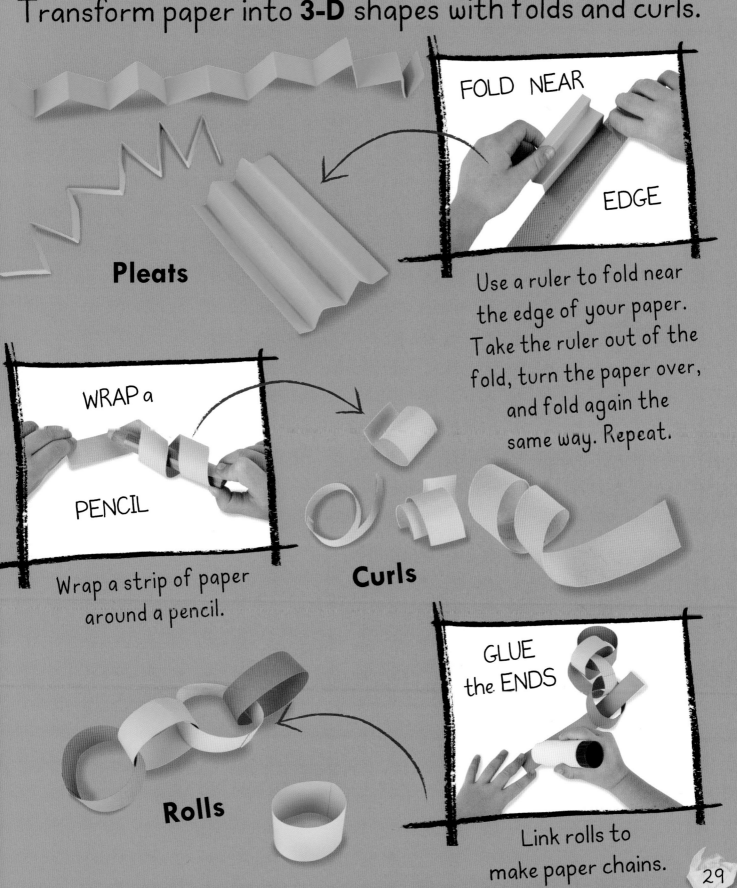

Pleats

FOLD NEAR

EDGE

Use a ruler to fold near the edge of your paper. Take the ruler out of the fold, turn the paper over, and fold again the same way. Repeat.

WRAP a

PENCIL

Wrap a strip of paper around a pencil.

Curls

GLUE the ENDS

Rolls

Link rolls to make paper chains.

29

Paper cutting

You can make some great paper effects with just a few snips here and there!

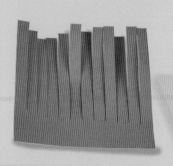

Fringes

SNIP to make a FRINGE

Make little snips along one edge of some paper. Don't cut all the way to the other side.

Draw a spiral to help you cut it out.

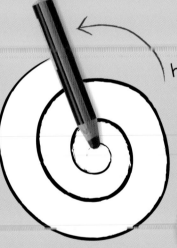

Spirals

CUT to

make a SPIRAL

Cut into the edge of a circle and keep cutting around and around working toward the middle.

Draw eyes on the middle of your spiral to make it into a curly snake!

Paper sculpture

Use your folding and cutting techniques to create a colorful paper sculpture.

Gather your paper creations.

What other paper shapes can you make?

onto thick card stock.

Glue your paper shapes...

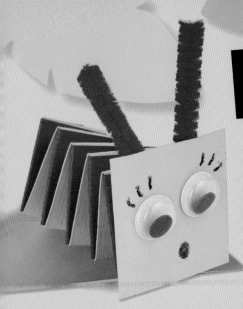

Paper
caterpillars

Make these cute caterpillars with just a bit of **folding** and **sticking**!

Tools needed:

Strips of colored paper

Pencil

Googly eyes

Glue

Safety scissors

Pipe cleaners

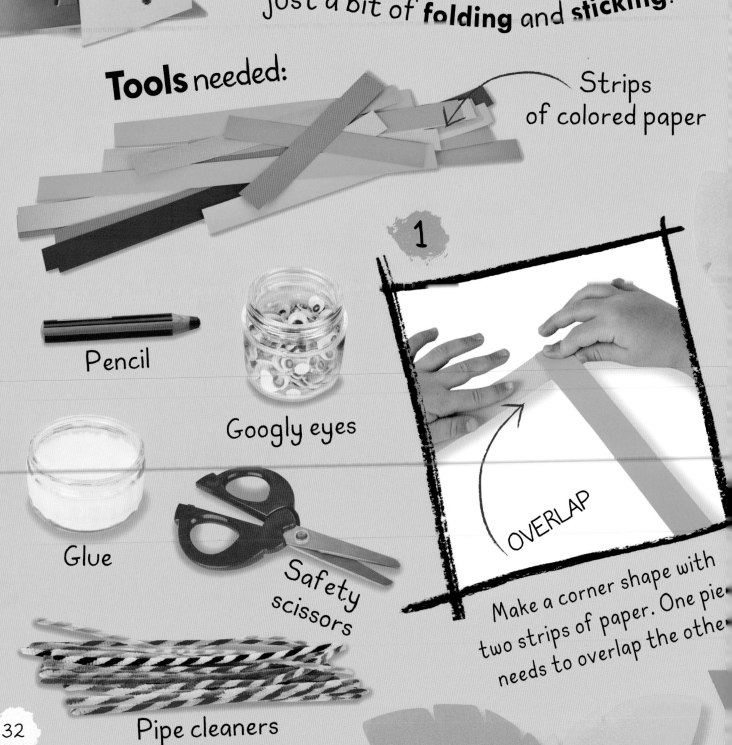

1

OVERLAP

Make a corner shape with two strips of paper. One piece needs to overlap the other.

2

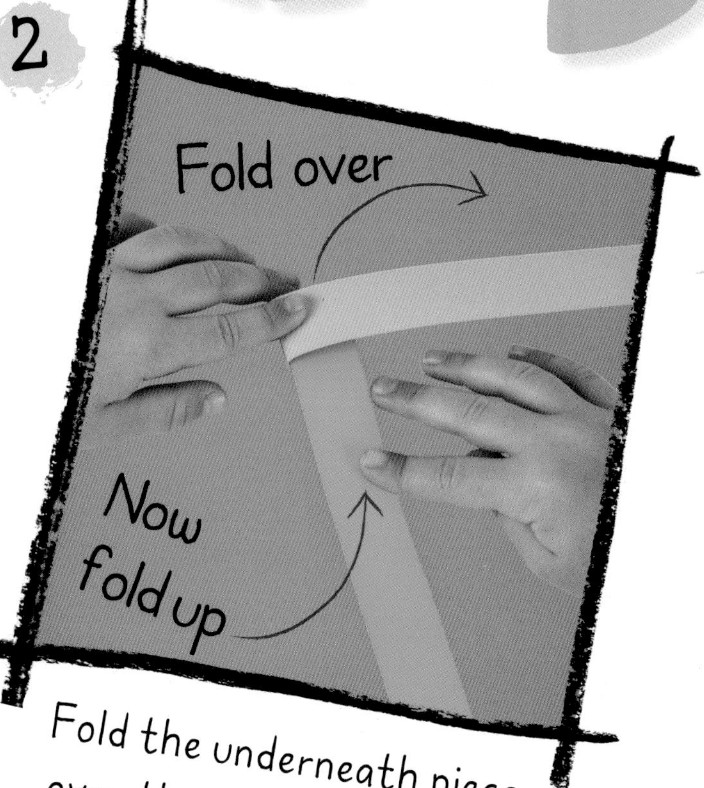

Fold over

Now fold up

Fold the underneath piece over the other strip. Now fold the other piece up and over in the same way.

3

Keep folding until you run out of paper.

Top tip
Always fold the underneath piece.

Pipe cleaner antennae

You have a super smile!

Googly eyes

Now make a face for your little critters.
Glue eyes and antennae onto a square piece of paper, and draw on a smile.

Stick the face to one end of the body.

Fan-tastic!

Keep cool on a hot day with these funny-face fans.

Tools needed:

Colored paper

Colored pencils

Pipe cleaners

Wood clothespins

Ribbons

Glue stick

Safety scissors

Ruler

1

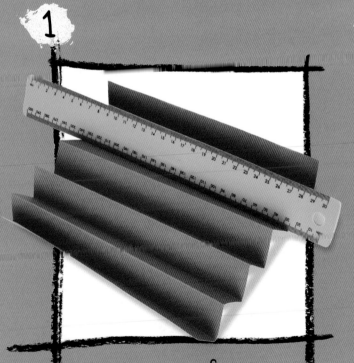

Fold a piece of paper using the pleating technique on page 29.

2

Draw an eye onto your pleated paper.

3 Fold and decorate another piece of paper in the same way.

4 Pinch the bottom edges of both pieces of paper together and slot into a peg.

5 Cut out a circle to make a nose. Glue it in the middle joining both pieces of paper.

6 Use a pipe cleaner to help hold the peg closed.

Top tip
These fans make great presents. Just add ribbons and gift tags.

Shadow puppets

Create a shadow scene with these easy-to-make **paper puppets.**

Tools needed:

Masking tape

Safety scissors

Black paper

White pencil

Straws

1

Top tip
Find templates in the front and back of the book to make your puppets.

Draw a puppet shape onto black paper and cut it out.

Attach a straw handle with tape.

Hold us up near a wall and shine a flashlight at us. Can you see our shadows?

Stained-glass elephant

Hang this elephant in a window and see how the sunlight shines through the thin tissue paper.

What other stained-glass animals should we make?

Tools needed:

Black card stock

Tissue paper strips

Felt-tip pen

Safety scissors   Glue stick

White pencil

Use the stencil from the front cover of the book to make your elephant.

1

CUT OUT

Draw around the elephant shape. Ask an adult to help you cut it out.

2

STICK

DOWN

Stick your strips of tissue paper over the elephant-shaped hole.

3

Draw an eye and an ear on your elephant with a black felt-tip pen.

Top tip
Decorate your picture with crumpled-up pieces of tissue paper.

Wet paper art

See how the colors **mix** and **run** when you spray water onto crepe paper.

Tools needed:

White paper
or card stock

Water spray
bottle

Crepe paper cut
into shapes

1

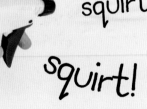

squirt!

squirt!

Spray water onto your
white paper.

2

ADD crepe shapes

Place your colored shapes
on the wet paper.

3

Top tip
Use lots of layers of wet crepe paper to make your picture extra colorful.

Look at how the colors run into one another.

When you have filled the white paper with colored shapes, spray more water on top.

4

When the crepe paper pieces are almost dry, peel them off.

Why not use your creation as wrapping paper?

Drawing and coloring

Practice your drawing skills and discover how to create different coloring effects.

What kind of picture should we draw?

Tools needed:

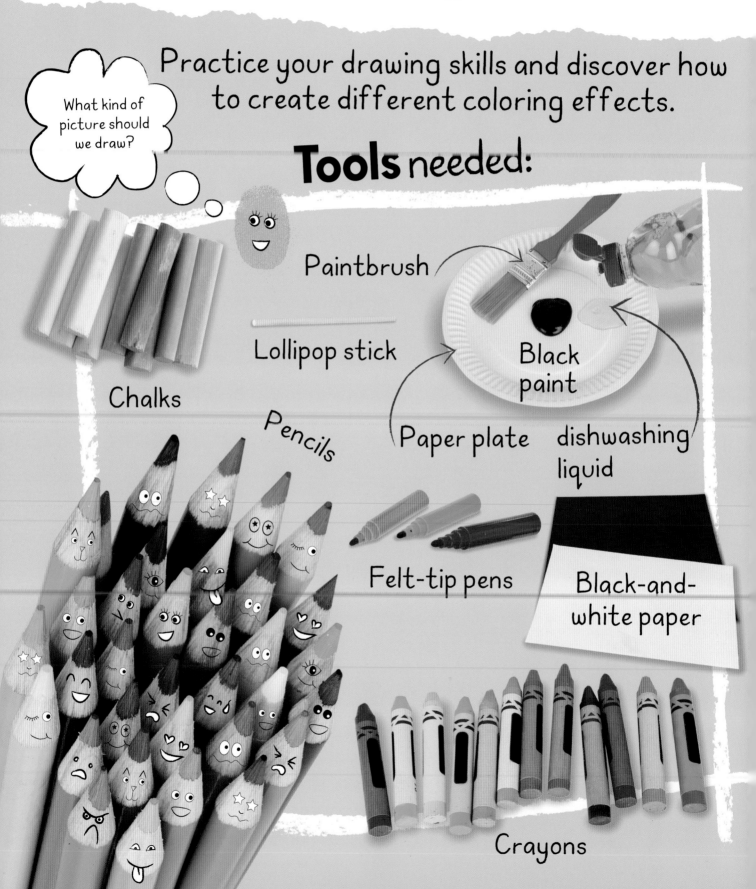

Paintbrush

Lollipop stick

Chalks

Pencils

Black paint

Paper plate

dishwashing liquid

Felt-tip pens

Black-and-white paper

Crayons

Use **pencils**, **pens**, **crayons**, or **chalk** to make lots of different **marks!**

Shading

Circles

Sparkle

Small circles

Dots

Zigzags

Spiral

Crosshatching

Dashes

Wiggles

Squiggles

Use a squiggle to draw my hair!

Draw a **picture** with just one **line.**

Keep your pencil on the paper, and don't stop!

Animal doodles

Learn to draw animals with these simple steps. Build your picture shape by shape.

Practice the shapes on scrap paper first.

Frankfurter dog

1 Draw a long frankfurter shape.

2 Now add a potato-shaped head, a tail, and four legs.

3 Finish off by adding ears, claws, and a face.

All this talk of frankfurters is making me hungry!

Sleepy cat

1

Draw a curved
bean shape.

2

Now add a round head.

3

Next, draw four
legs and a tail.

4

To finish, add ears,
claws, and a face. Don't
forget the whiskers!

Singing bird

1

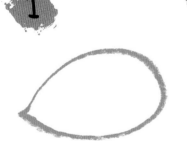

Draw a
balloon shape.

2

Next add leaf-shaped
feathers for a tail, and a
small balloon-shaped wing.

3

Finally, give your bird
legs, eyes, feet—and a
beak so it can sing!

45

Chalk art

Create your own **cheery chalky aliens.**

What planet are they from?

Try rubbing chalk on its side.

Chalk looks great on black paper. Try drawing on sidewalks, too!

Top tip
Go over the top of chalk marks with a watery paintbrush to blend the chalk lines.

Give your alien antennae and a funny face with lots of eyes.

I don't understand his language...

"BURLIBUB FOMMIT!"

Chalk

Scratch art magic!

See colors appear as if by magic with scratch art drawings.

WOW! It must be magic!

Tools needed:

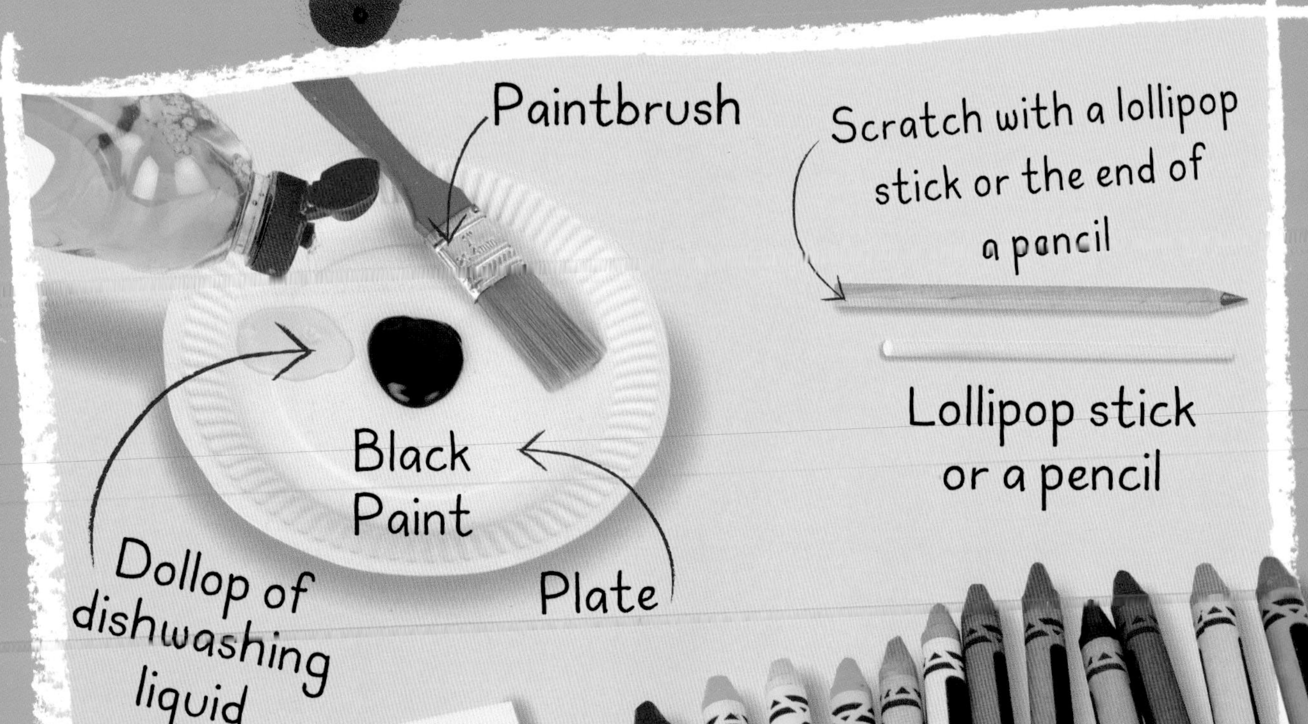

Paintbrush

Scratch with a lollipop stick or the end of a pencil

Black Paint

Lollipop stick or a pencil

Dollop of dishwashing liquid

Plate

Paper

Crayons

1

Color a pattern onto a piece of paper. Use lots of colors.

2

Mix the black paint and dishwashing liquid together. Paint over your crayon picture and let dry.

3

Scratch a drawing into the black paint.

Top tip
The more colors you use, the more magical your picture will look!

Lollipop stick

49

Make and create

Turn ordinary household items into amazing art.

Color matching game

Practice your colors with this fun **game**. You'll need your color wheel from page 11.

1

Cut out each section of your color wheel.

2

Go on a hunt for colored objects!

3

Match your objects to the color of each section.

So colorful!

A tower of **tubes**

Paint cardboard tubes and slot them together to make a towering fort.

How high can you build your towers?

1

Cut cardboard tubes into different lengths.

Paint your tubes in bright colors.

2

Add windows and patterns with white paint.

3

Cut two slits at the top and bottom, and slot your tubes together.

Rainbow mobile

Create a colorful cardboard mobile.

Tools needed:

 Red Orange Yellow

 Green Blue Indigo Violet

Paints

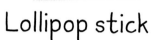 Lollipop stick

 String

 Safety scissors

 Wood beads

Felt-tip pen

Corrugated cardboard

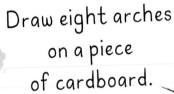 Paintbrush

1 Draw eight arches on a piece of cardboard.

2

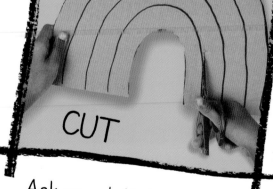

CUT

Ask an adult to help you cut along the lines. You should be left with seven arches.

54

3

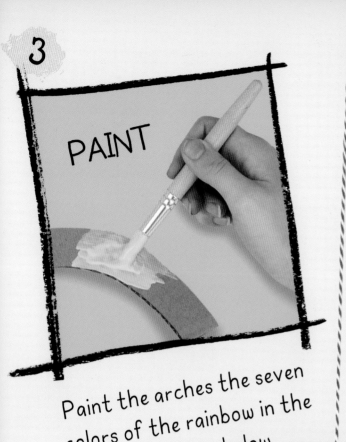

PAINT

Paint the arches the seven colors of the rainbow in the order shown below.

4

Lollipop stick

THREAD string

Ask an adult to help you poke a length of string through the top of each arch from biggest to smallest.

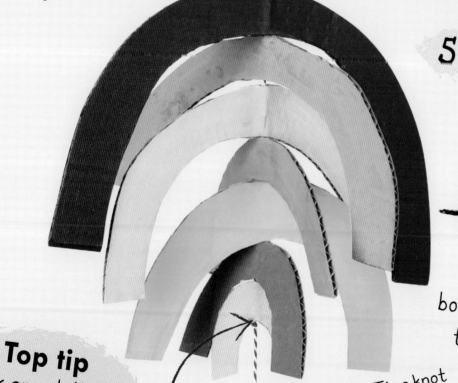

5

THREAD

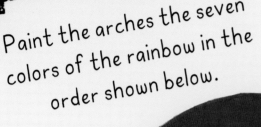

Thread some beads on the bottom of the string to weigh it down.

Top tip
Ask an adult to help you hang your mobile in your bedroom.

Tie a knot here.

Tie a knot here.

Tie a knot here.

Watch it spin!

55

Magical unicorn

Find head, horn, and ear templates at the back of the book.

Make your own magical, fantastical unicorn hobbyhorse!

Tools needed:

Turn to page 30 to see how to make card-stock fringe.

Fringed, colored card stock

Stapler

Horn cut from sparkly card stock

Glue stick

Safety scissors

Pencil

Horse-head shapes

Cut two head shapes out of white card stock.

Ears

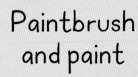

Paintbrush and paint

Long cardboard tube

1

PAINT your cardboard TUBE

Paint your tube in a nice bright color. This will be your unicorn's handle.

2

Glue around the edges of both head shapes but not the bottom of the neck. Stick the fringed card stock, ears, and horn between the two.

Draw me a face and give me fringed card-stock eyelashes.

3

Staple the two head shapes at each corner of the neck. Push the tube up through the space in the middle.

Gallop around on your magical unicorn!

Top tip
Why not glue on glitter and sequins for extra magical sparkle?

57

Shadow theater

Make a theater and put on a **shadow show** with your **puppets** from page 36.

Tools needed:

Ruler

Lamp

Glue

Cardboard box

Safety scissors

Masking tape

Felt-tip pen

Tracing or parchment paper

Hold us up at the back of the theater.

1

Cut away one of the long sides of the box.

Draw a rectangle on your box. It should be about the width of a ruler away from the edges.

2

CUT

Ask an adult to help you cut out the rectangle.

3

Tape tracing paper to the inside of the box covering the hole.

Light your theater from behind with a lamp.

4

Cut out and decorate pillars and a pediment. Glue them to the front of the theater.

59

Cardboard collage

Make a city scene with scraps of **paper, fabric, and cardboard.**

Tools needed:

Googly eyes

Paintbrush for glue

Paints

Paintbrush

Cardboard, colored paper, and fabric scraps

Tinfoil

Masking tape   Glue

Scissors

Felt-tip pens

Shiny **fish**

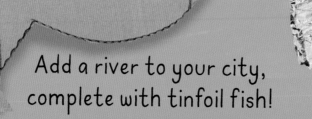

Add a river to your city, complete with tinfoil fish!

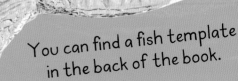

You can find a fish template in the back of the book.

City scene

Cut out your cardboard shapes and glue on your paper and fabric pieces.

Paint window panes and other details.

Use colored masking tape to create windows.

Use different materials for doors.

Patterned paper can look fun, too.

Use felt-tip pens to decorate us.

Glue on googly eyes.

61

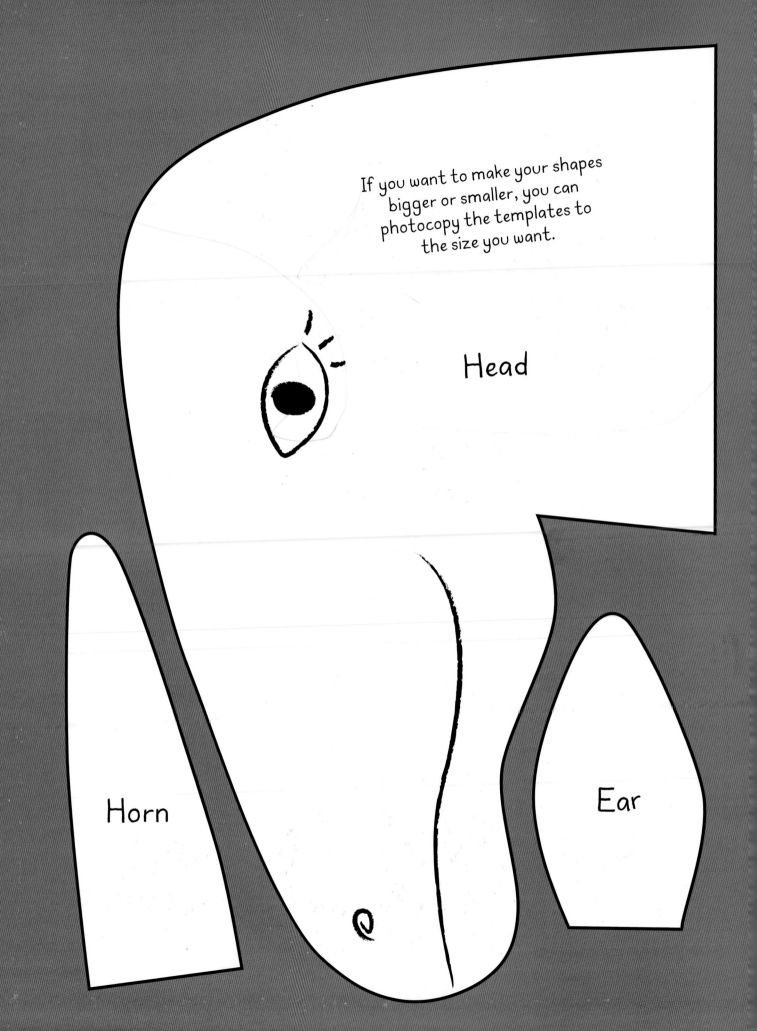

If you want to make your shapes bigger or smaller, you can photocopy the templates to the size you want.

Head

Horn

Ear

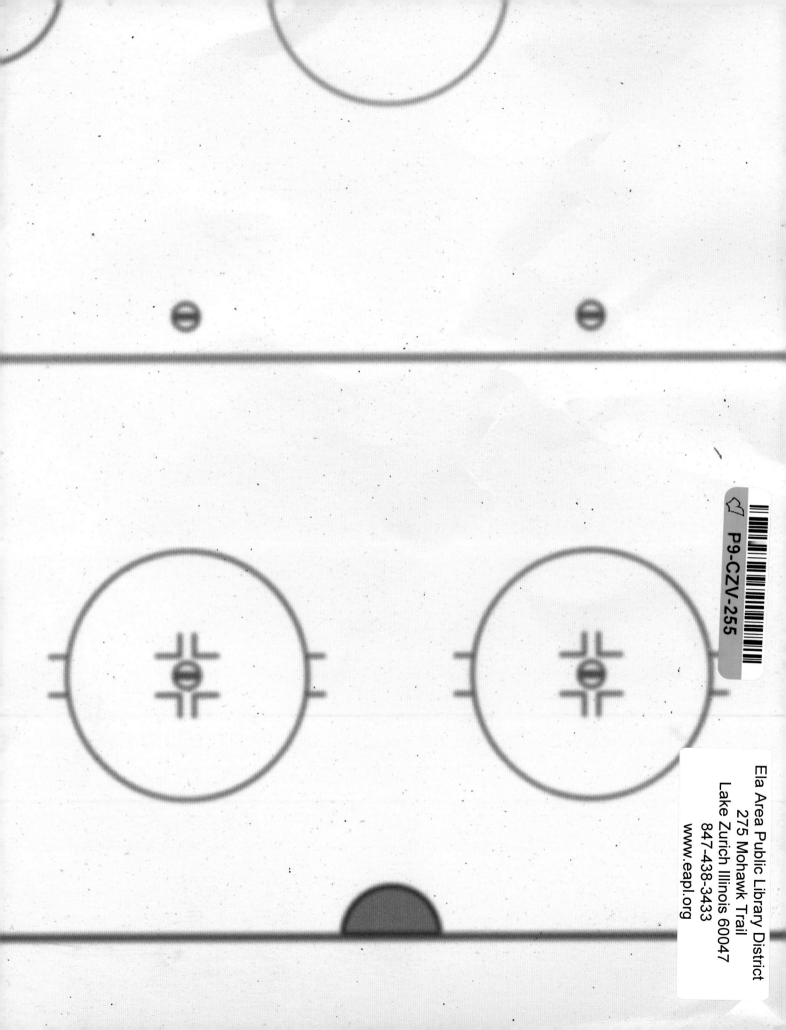

HOCKEY

Then to WOW!

Sports Illustrated KIDS

This early cable-knit uniform—an actual "hockey sweater"—was worn by players on Team Canada during the 1928 Olympics.

THEN

Adidas designed Team Canada's jersey for the 2016 World Cup of Hockey. It is made of lightweight synthetic fabrics that are also durable.

Managing Editor, SPORTS ILLUSTRATED KIDS **Mark Bechtel**

Writer **Sam Page**

Designer **Beth Bugler**

Editor **Sarah Kwak**

Photo Editor **Abigail Nichols**

Copy Editor **Pamela Ann Roberts**

Reporter: **Jeremy Fuchs**

Production Manager **Hillary Leary**

Illustrations by **Andrew Roberts**

ISBN: 978-1-68330-011-3
Library of Congress Control Number: 2017939415

First edition, 2017
1 TLF 17
1 3 5 7 9 8 6 4 2

We welcome your comments and suggestions about Time Inc. Books.
Please write to us at:

Time Inc. Books
Attention: Book Editors
P.O. Box 62310
Tampa, FL 33662-2310
(800) 765-6400

timeincbooks.com

Time Inc. Books products may be purchased for business or promotional use. For information on bulk purchases, please contact Christi Crowley in the Special Sales Department at (845) 895-9858.

CONTENTS

Hockey, like baseball, evolved from several similar games originally played on grass in the British Isles. When the sport crossed the Atlantic, it quickly took hold in Canada, particularly in Montreal, where people began playing field hockey on ice with a flat piece of wood in lieu of a ball in the 1870s.

Since that time, techniques, equipment, rules, and even fashion have evolved as the game extended its reach across the globe. Still, much of that 19th-century game is recognizable today.

The Rules

How the game has been played

Hockey used to be a simpler game: He skates, he shoots, he scores. Now it usually takes more to earn a goal. He skates, he dumps the puck in deep, he chases it into the corner and dekes a defender. . . . The game has evolved thanks to rule changes meant to make the game more exciting and to raise scoring. From the forward pass to video review, a lot has changed.

1934

The league introduces penalty shots for players who are tripped while attempting to score. The shots were restricted to a circular area about 40 feet from the goalmouth.

1929

Forward passing is allowed in the offensive zone, dramatically increasing scoring.

1918

The NHL adds two blue lines to the ice, which create the offensive, defensive, and neutral zones. Forward passes which had been illegal, are allowed in the neutral zone to speed up play.

1917

Goalies are allowed to fall on the ice to make saves; previously, they were assessed a minor penalty or a two-dollar fine.

1910

Thirty-minute halves are replaced by three 20-minute periods.

1877

The *Montreal Gazette* publishes rules for ice hockey, copied almost entirely from a field hockey rule book.

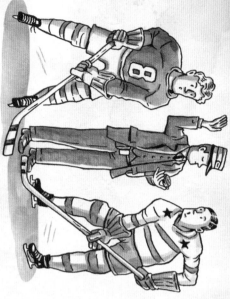

1937

Overtime is abolished in the regular season so that games can end on time. (Trains were on tight schedules because of WWII.)

Players serving minor penalties get released when an opponent scores with the man advantage. This rule comes after Montreal Canadiens star center Jean Béliveau scores a hat trick during a single power play.

1941

Icing rules, which forbid teams from clearing the puck the length of the ice, are instituted.

Players are allowed to skate toward the net on penalty shots.

1942

1943

The NHL introduces the center-ice red line, which allows for breakout passes from the defensive zone.

1956

1976

To curb an increasingly rowdy game, the instigator penalty is created for players who start fights.

1979

Helmets become mandatory for all new skaters entering the league. Older players, grandfathered in under the rule, weren't required to wear a lid. Craig MacTavish, a rookie in 1979–1980, retires as the last helmetless player in 1997.

Video replay starts for questionable goal calls.

1983

Overtime returns with a sudden-death five-minute period at the end of tied games. In 2005, the NHL adds a three-round shootout to settle games undecided through OT.

1991

Players can now pass from deep in their defensive zone all the way up to the opposing team's blue line, as the NHL abandoned what was known as the two-line pass rule. Goaltenders can no longer play the puck in the corners behind their net. They can only make passes from a trapezoid-shaped area directly behind the goal.

2005

skates

From bones strapped to shoes to sleek carbon-fiber marvels, hockey footwear has come a long way

■ 1800s ■

Until the 20th century, metal skates resembled the bone predecessors in one important way: They had to be strapped onto the soles of shoes. By the time the NHL got started, the skate-boot combo had become standard.

■ 3000 B.C. ■

O.K., so they weren't used for hockey, but the earliest ice skates appeared some 5,000 years ago. Made of bones—usually from a horse—these prototype skates helped the people of what is now Finland traverse frozen lakes during the daytime. By digging into the ice, the bones provided stability on the slippery surface. This early skating method was more efficient than walking. Scientists found that even these primitive models, which didn't move very fast, conserved people's energy on the flat terrain of Scandinavia.

⚡ 1970s ⚡

This skate, worn by Morris Mott of the now-defunct California Golden Seals, was part of the CCM Super Tacks line, which continues today and is advertised as providing superior fit and rigidity. The bright color, which matched the Golden Seals' jerseys, was unusual, even at the time.

⚡ 1950s ⚡

The skate began to evolve and took a more recognizable shape with a blade holder and a high ankle boot. In this era, blades, also called runners, were flat along the bottom; in contrast, today's skates are sharpened with a slightly hollow groove to improve grip on the ice.

⚡ Current ⚡

Today's skates feature all sorts of bells and whistles. This one boasts a carbon outsole to reduce its weight, a pump around the ankle to increase snugness, and a carbon-coated steel blade to improve grip. Pairs these days can cost nearly $1,000.

Stick

How hockey's two most basic pieces of equipment have become increasingly complex

1800S

The earliest ice hockey sticks were carved from single pieces of wood and resembled field hockey twigs, due to their short curved heads. But before long, the more familiar long blade became standard. Hornbeam, birch, and maple were the most popular types of wood used.

1930S

By the 1930s, sticks were made from two or three pieces of wood, which were glued together. They mostly worked well, except that sometimes cold temperatures caused the glue to come undone.

1960S

Chicago Blackhawks forwards Stan Mikita and Bobby Hull experimented with curving their stick blades in the 1960s. The "banana blade," named for its shape, caused shots to act unpredictably in the air. It paid off for Hull, who led the league in goals seven times. But in 1967 the NHL made a rule that limited curves to 1½ inches. Today, curves cannot exceed ¾ of an inch.

1990s

Wayne Gretzky popularized the aluminum stick when he began using the Easton HXP 5100 in 1990. The durable metal shafts had just the right amount of give, and as an added bonus, they were much lighter than their wooden counterparts.

2000s

Going back to the hockey stick's roots, one-piece sticks have again become the NHL standard. But now, instead of wood, they are made of carbon fiber, or fiberglass, a strong but flexible material that allows players to shoot harder.

PUCK

THEN

Traditional field hockey balls were too dangerous on ice because they bounced too much, so the flatter puck was introduced for the first indoor ice hockey game in 1875. Pucks, which were carved from wood, didn't bounce as much and were much easier for players to handle.

NOW

Measuring three inches in diameter and one inch thick, the modern puck is made of a variety of ingredients, including rubber, two kinds of oils, sulfur, and antioxidants. The disks are also frozen before games to make them slide better and bounce less.

Sweaters

1962–1963

For the first half of the 1960s, the Bruins had three jerseys in their wardrobe: white, black, and gold.

1948–1949

In the 1930s, teams embraced simplicity. Instead of uniforms with the full team name stitched across the front, the Bruins went with an easy "B."

Boston introduced the original version of its spoked "B" as a 25th-anniversary logo (represented by the years '24 and '49 on either side of the letter).

1930s

1928–1929

The tradition of calling hockey jerseys *sweaters* comes from hockey's earliest days, when they were exactly that. The Bruins wore this striped pullover when they won their first Stanley Cup.

Charting the trends in NHL jerseys through one of the league's most iconic franchises

Bobby Orr wore this black uniform when he scored his famous "flying goal" against the St. Louis Blues to win the 1970 Stanley Cup. The sweater's collar featured laces, which Orr removed.

1969–1970

The Bruins added a secondary bear-head logo as a shoulder patch. Lace-up collars were replaced with a black V-neck, and player names were added to the backs.

1980s

The Bruins introduced a fresh set of black, white, and gold jerseys as they moved into a new home arena—TD Garden. These uniforms featured a patch for the 1996 NHL All-Star Game in Boston.

1990s

A far cry from the wool pullovers of the early years, modern jerseys feature lightweight, sweat-wicking polyester. But the Bruins' jersey features throwback elements, like a collar tie.

2010s

Goalie

What started out as a safety measure has turned into an artful form of expression

= 1970s =

Minding the net for the Soviet Union in the 1972 Summit Series against Canada, Vladislav Tretiak popularized the plastic helmet and metal cage, a precursor to the modern mask.

= 1960s =

This decade saw two lasting innovations to goalie mask design. The Boston Bruins' Gerry Cheevers became the first player to decorate his shield. The team's trainer drew on stitches to mark the places where pucks would have injured the goalie (*left*). Meanwhile, others adopted "pretzel" masks (*below*), which more closely resemble today's cages.

= 1959 =

After being hit in the nose by a shot early in a November game, Montreal Canadiens goalie Jacques Plante returned to the bench with a few stitches and a proposition for coach Toe Blake: *I can go back into the game, but I have to wear my practice mask.* Blake didn't care for the look and thought the goalie would wear it only for one or game, but after Plante won the Vezina Trophy and backstopped Montreal to a Stanley Cup while wearing it, the mask was here to stay.

= 1930s =

The earliest goalie masks were worn occasionally and only out of necessity. Clint Benedict was the first NHLer to don a face guard (*below, left*) after he broke his nose during the 1929–1930 season. Team Japan's Teiji Honma wore a mask (*right*) to protect his glasses at the 1936 Olympics.

Masks

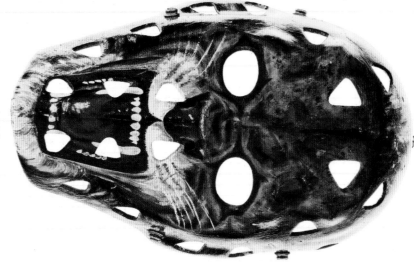

= 1976 =

A zany character off the ice, the New York Rangers' Gilles Gratton found a way to express himself on it when he commissioned a wild mask, which was inspired by a photo he had seen in *National Geographic*.

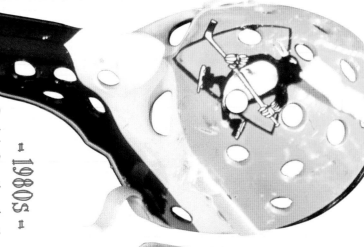

= 1980s =

Back before the plastic protective throat guard became popular, Pittsburgh Penguin Michel Dion wore this unique mask. The long duck bill shape offered maximal coverage of one of the most vulnerable parts of the body.

= 1990s =

By the 1990s, goalie masks were much more than just masks, as players turned to modern fiberglass helmets with a metal cage to protect their faces. Also standard was the painting of the helmets, like Brian Hayward's classic shark head.

= 2010s =

These days, netminders obsess over mask design, even getting one-off helmets custom-painted for special games. Montreal Canadiens goalie Carey Price's bucket for the 2011 Heritage Classic fittingly paid tribute to his predecessors by looking like a face wearing an old-school mask.

Goalie Pads

From big leather pillows to futuristic body armor, no set of hockey equipment has changed more—or been the subject of more debate

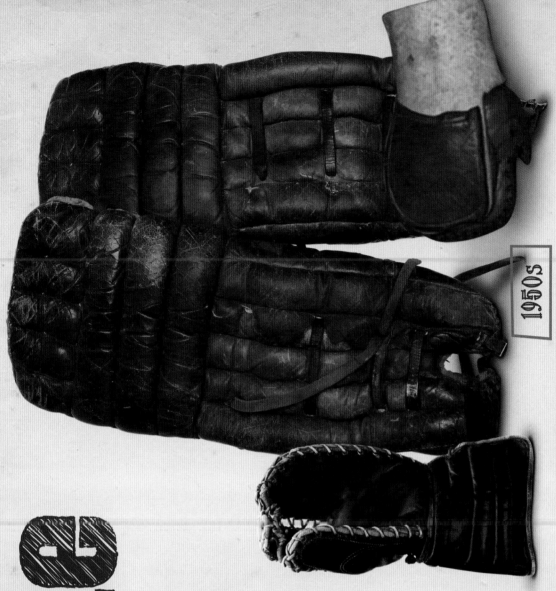

1950s

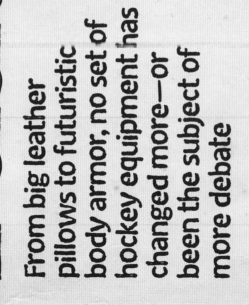

Early leg pads were modeled after cricket pads (which are closer to a baseball catcher's shin guards in size). These "pillows" were made from horsehide and filled with furniture stuffing. But they were heavy, especially when they became waterlogged with melted ice and sweat. Goalie gloves, which looked like modified five-finger baseball mitts, came to resemble a first baseman's glove, with a large pocket that made it easier to catch the puck. Blockers, boards worn over the goalie's other hand, were made of wood frames filled with sponge or rubber.

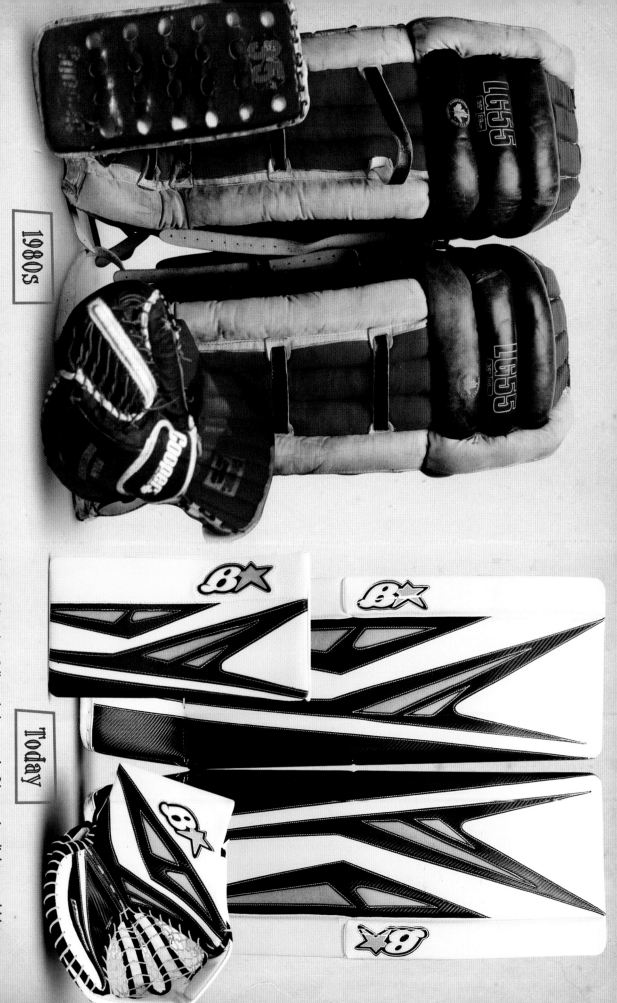

1980s

Synthetic leather material made all padding lighter and more waterproof. That meant goalies could wear larger pads—taller leg guards and a wider catching glove—to cover more of the net without being weighed down. High-density foam also improved body protection drastically during this era. Instead of wearing baseball catcher–style chest protectors and padded shirts, goalies could fit firm, lightweight body armor under their jerseys. This technology also improved the blocker pad.

Today

Modern padding has followed the trend of becoming lighter and bigger. Leg pads no longer feature stuffed rolls. Their shape and size allow goalies to close the space between their legs—the five hole—when they drop to their knees in the now-popular butterfly technique. Their shorts also have padding around the thighs and waist. Since goalies today block so much of the net, which hasn't changed in size, the NHL introduced pad size limits before the 2013–2014 season in an attempt to give shooters more open areas to score.

Arenas

Indoors and out, the homes of hockey's past and present have taken many shapes

Opened in 1924, the Montreal Forum was the successor to a roller rink of the same name. The Forum, which would host the Canadiens for 70 seasons, cost 1.5 million Canadian dollars to build (more than $21 million today), and the team hit the ice just five months after it broke ground. By contrast, the Edmonton Oilers' Rogers Place (*right*), which opened in September 2016, cost more than 600 million Canadian dollars and took more than two years to build.

The exterior of Montreal's Forum, rectangular in shape with a triangular roof, made it resemble a church or a barn rather than the rounded arenas you see today. The Canadiens and the Montreal Maroons combined for 24 Stanley Cups while playing there. The building, which was renovated in 1968, hosted its final NHL game—a 4–1 Canadiens win over the Dallas Stars—on March 11, 1996. The Forum has since been converted into a shopping mall and movie theater.

= THEN =

Price of Admission

Edmonton's Rogers Place can hold 18,641 fans for hockey games and more than 20,000 people for concerts. Some individual tickets in the lower bowl for Oilers games during the arena's opening season cost more than 300 Canadian dollars.

Seeing Clearly

Weighing in at 90,000 pounds, the Rogers Place scoreboard is the biggest of its kind in the NHL. Its centerpiece is a high-definition screen that is 46 feet wide and 36 feet tall. It is so big that fans in the front row can't see the main screen from their seats. To help them out, there are smaller ones embedded in the scoreboard's base.

Get Appy

In addition to its scoreboard, Rogers Place features plenty of technology meant to enhance the fan experience. The arena has more than 1,200 TVs and free Wi-Fi Internet access at all levels. Fans can also download an app for their smartphones that allows them to purchase tickets, check team stats, and more.

⸗NOW⸗

« THEN »
On Ponds

Outdoor hockey predates its indoor counterpart by years—maybe even centuries. One of the earliest outdoor games played by an NHL team happened on February 2, 1954 at Marquette Branch Prison, a maximum-security penitentiary in Michigan's Upper Peninsula. At the warden's invitation, the Red Wings, who would go on to win the Stanley Cup that season, played a game against the prisoners. The Wings led 18—0 after the first period.

Arena Design Over the Years

« 1931 »

Maple Leaf Gardens, n downtown Toronto, is a rectangular hall. These were the standard during the era of the Original Six teams.

« 1958 »

Famed architect Eero Saarinen designed Ingalls Rink at Yale. Saarinen's other works include St. Louis's Gateway Arch.

« 1967 »

The Spectrum, the former home of the Philadelphia Flyers, was an early example of the rounded arenas popular today.

= NOW =
In Stadiums

The NHL returned to the great outdoors with the 2003 Heritage Classic, played between the Oilers and the Canadiens at Edmonton's Commonwealth Stadium. The temperatures that day reached as low as —4°F, but the game was an extremely hot ticket. Five years later, the NHL created its annual Winter Classic, played around New Year's Day. The 2014 Classic at Ann Arbor's Michigan Stadium (*right*), set an NHL attendance record with 105,491 spectators.

= 1983 =

The Scotiabank Saddledome, which was built on Calgary's Stampede Grounds, is actually named for the shape of its roof.

= 1989 =

Ericsson Globe, located in Stockholm, Sweden, was designed to be a replica of the sun—just 20 million times smaller.

= 2008 =

The Majori Primary School Sports Hall in Jurmale, Latvia, is 60% translucent. You can watch a game from outside!

Player Origins

UNITED STATES
6.7%

UNITED KINGDOM
4.4%

CANADA
88.9%

1917–1918

The NHL was predominantly Canadian in the league's first season—to an extent that even this puck chart undersells. Since there were only 45 players in 1917–1918, the 4.4% that represents Brits amounted to only two players, both of whom had lived and played in Canada before the NHL was founded.

One of them—Hall of Famer Joe Hall—grew up in Manitoba. The other, Ken Thompson, played just one game. The three Americans, who made up 6.7% of the league, only accounted for 1.2% of the points scored. In the 1920s and 1930s, the NHL would add players from Europe. But it truly became an international league in 1989–1990, when the best players from Russia joined.

Hockey is played anywhere there is natural ice—and even some places where there isn't. Once almost exclusively North American, the NHL is now a global community

The 2015–2016 season was the first time Canadians did not make up the majority of the NHL. That season, 49.0% came from the Great White North. The number of players from Sweden and Finland, meanwhile, continues to grow.

Five years ago, Swedes and Finns made up less than 10% of the league; in 2015–2016, they accounted for 13.7%. The United States has made similar gains, going from 18.9% a decade ago to about 25% today. These trends were reflected in the 2016 NHL draft, when an American and a Finn went one-two, and only two of the top 10 picks grew up in Canada.

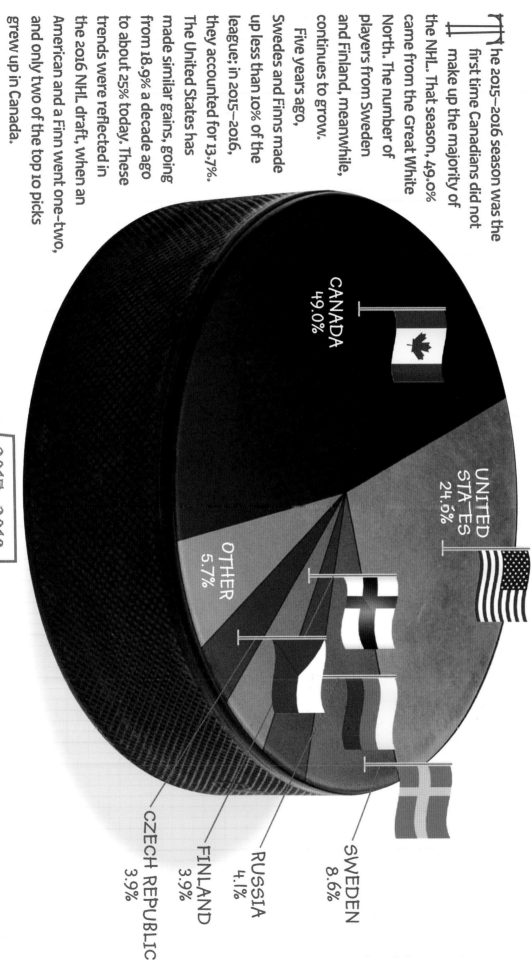

2015–2016

CANADA
49.0%

UNITED STATES
24.5%

OTHER
5.7%

SWEDEN
8.6%

RUSSIA
4.1%

FINLAND
3.9%

CZECH REPUBLIC
3.9%

Combining the grace of figure skating, the toughness of boxing, and the hand-eye coordination of baseball, no sport demands more from its participants than ice hockey. That's why the game attracts such a wide array of talents—and personalities.

Hockey's stars have found plenty of ways to stand out over the years. Whether it's for their jaw-dropping skills on the ice or their head-turning style off it, here are the players who stood out the most.

playmakers

With superior vision and the skills to execute a plan, these players were the best at anticipating moves and creating goals

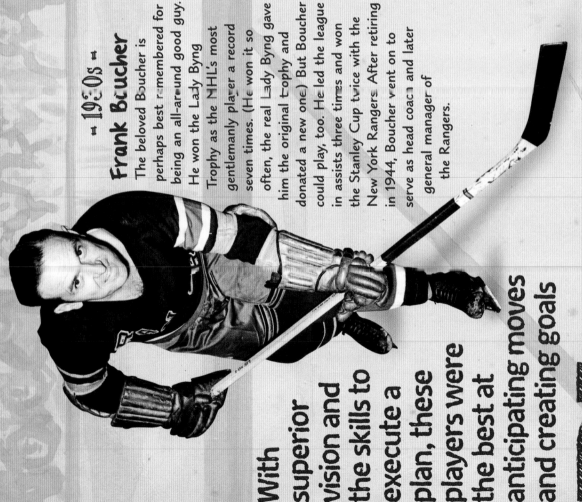

▪ 1930s ▪
Frank Boucher

The beloved Boucher is perhaps best remembered for being an all-around good guy. He won the Lady Byng Trophy as the NHL's most gentlemanly player a record seven times. (He won it so often, the real Lady Byng gave him the original trophy and donated a new one.) But Boucher could play, too. He led the league in assists three times and won the Stanley Cup twice with the New York Rangers. After retiring in 1944, Boucher went on to serve as head coach and later general manager of the Rangers.

▪ 1940s ▪
Bill Cowley

An early example of the many skills that later became synonymous with playmakers, Cowley had great on-ice vision, anticipation, stickhandling, and passing abilities. The two-time Hart Trophy winner led the league in assists three times. In 1939, he chipped in 11 helpers in 12 playoff games as his Boston Bruins won the Stanley Cup. At the time of his retirement, he was the NHL's all-time points leader with 548.

= 1950s =
Gordie Howe

Mr. Hockey could do it all: score goals (he had 801 in his NHL career), stay healthy (he played until he was 51), and be tough (1,685 career penalty minutes). So it's no surprise he could also make his teammates better. The rare winger on this list, Howe played on the Detroit Red Wings' Production Line with left wing Ted Lindsay and center Sid Abel. With that unit, Howe led the league in assists three times and won four Stanley Cups. A model for future playmakers, Howe posed a threat, whether he passed or shot. When he retired, Howe had 2,358 points (in the NHL and WHA combined), a total that has only been surpassed by Wayne Gretzky.

= 1960s =
Stan Mikita

Teaming up with Bobby Hull on the Chicago Blackhawks, Mikita was part of one of the best scoring duos in NHL history, and he led the league in total points four times. Entering the NHL as a teenager, the center weighed just 152 pounds and served plenty of penalty minutes as he tried to prove his toughness. Later on, bigger and older, Mikita reformed his game and became one of the league's least-penalized players. That change led him to become the first player ever to earn the Hart Trophy, the Lady Byng, and a first-team All-Star selection in the same season—in 1966–1967. He would repeat that trifecta the following year.

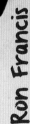

= 1980s =
Wayne Gretzky

Equipped with an innate awareness of his teammates' whereabouts on the ice, Gretzky always seemed one step ahead of defenders. Often setting up linemate Jari Kurri, the Great One also loved to slow play down with the puck on his stick, most famously behind the net, which became known as Gretzky's Office. He scored or assisted on 200 or more goals four times in his career, totals that modern-day top lines can only dream about. His career 2,857 points in the NHL is sports' most unbreakable record.

= 1970s =
Bryan Trottier

Not the fastest, biggest, or most skilled player, Trottier distinguished himself with his hard work, tenacity, and intelligence. A second-round pick in 1974, he scored 95 points as a 19-year-old, winning the Calder Trophy as the league's best rookie the following season. From there, he would go on to score more than 100 points six times. The anchor of the New York Islanders that won four straight Stanley Cups during the early 1980s, Trottier had 29 points in 21 games during the 1980 postseason, when he took home the Conn Smythe Trophy as playoff MVP.

Ron Francis

Because he played in the same era as Gretzky and Mario Lemieux, Francis is often overlooked. But the underrated center quietly amassed the second-most assists in NHL history, behind only Gretzky. Francis holds virtually every record for the Hartford Whalers franchise, which became the Carolina Hurricanes in 1997. He also won two Stanley Cups with the Penguins. In 1995–1996 he led the league with 92 assists, setting up superstars Lemieux and Jaromir Jagr.

Golden Age of Playmaking

= 1990s =

Mario Lemieux

Standing 6'4" and weighing 230 pounds, Lemieux dominated with his unrivaled skill set. Defenders were often rendered helpless as the big-bodied Lemieux drove past them. He ended Gretzky's streak of eight consecutive Hart Trophies in 1987-1988, and then scored a career-high 199 points the following season. If not for his health problems, Lemieux may have challenged the Great One's records.

Adam Oates

The 1989 trade that sent Oates to the St. Louis Blues brought together a perfect match because Oates, a player who loved to pass, got to play with Brett Hull, a player who loved to shoot. Together, Oates and Hull were reminiscent of another old dangerous scoring duo: Chicago's Mikita and Brett's dad, Bobby. But Oates enjoyed just as much success without his Blues wingman. The center led the NHL in assists while playing with the Boston Bruins, the Washington Capitals and the Philadelphia Flyers.

= 2000s =

Joe Thorton

Known as Jumbo Joe, the 6'4" Thornton has managed to put up gaudy offensive totals even in the lower-scoring modern era. Traded to the San Jose Sharks by the Boston Bruins during the 2005-2006 season, Thornton finished the season with 96 assists, 125 points, and the Hart Trophy. He would top 90 helpers again the following year—a mark no player has reached since. Among active players, he trails only the ageless Jagr in points.

snipers

= 1940s =
Maurice Richard

"Rocket" Richard became the NHL's first 50-goal scorer during the 1944–1945 season, which was just 50 games long. At the time of his retirement after the 1960 season, the Montreal Canadiens' star had scored a record-setting 544 goals. The trophy given annually to the league's top goal scorer is named in his honor.

= 1950s =
Gordie Howe

The Red Wings' franchise player had a complete offensive game (page 29), and shooting was a big part of it. He led the league in goals five times and is one of just two players with more than 800 points, despite spending six seasons in the rival World Hockey Association.

= 1960s =
Bobby Hull

Using a powerful slap shot with one of the league's first curved stick blades, the Golden Jet launched shots that were fast and erratic. He led the NHL in goals seven times as a Chicago Blackhawk and also set the WHA's single-season record with 77 goals in 1974–1975.

= 1970s =
Phil Esposito

Not the most physically gifted player, Esposito figured out a simple formula for scoring: Stand in front of the net and shoot . . . a lot. His 550 shots in 1970–1971 remain a single-season record and resulted in 76 goals.

¤ 1980s ¤
Mike Bossy

In 1980–1981, the shifty Islanders winger became the first player since Richard to score 50 goals in 50 games. In his 10 NHL seasons, Bossy scored 60 goals five times, had a record nine straight 50-goal seasons, and scored 85 times in the playoffs.

¤ 1990s ¤
Brett Hull

Like his father, Bobby, Brett had a golden touch around the net. Though not a heralded prospect, Hull still developed into a dominant scorer. His 86 goals in 1990–1991 with the Blues is the most by any player other than Wayne Gretzky. And in 1999, he scored the Cup-winning goal for Dallas.

¤ 2000s ¤
Pavel Bure

Bure had a great shot, but he often didn't need it. His blazing speed led to countless breakaway chances. Fooling the goaltender with a quick deke, Bure could simply tap the puck into an empty net. He had consecutive 60-goal seasons with the Canucks in the early 1990s.

¤ 2010s ¤
Alexander Ovechkin

Ovechkin possesses perhaps the quickest wrister in NHL history. Able to get his shot off even with the defense all over him, Washington's Great 8 is the only player besides Esposito to get 500 shots on goal in a single season. Just 31, Ovechkin has already led the league in goals six times.

Putting the biscuit in the basket is the whole point of the game. These guys did it the best

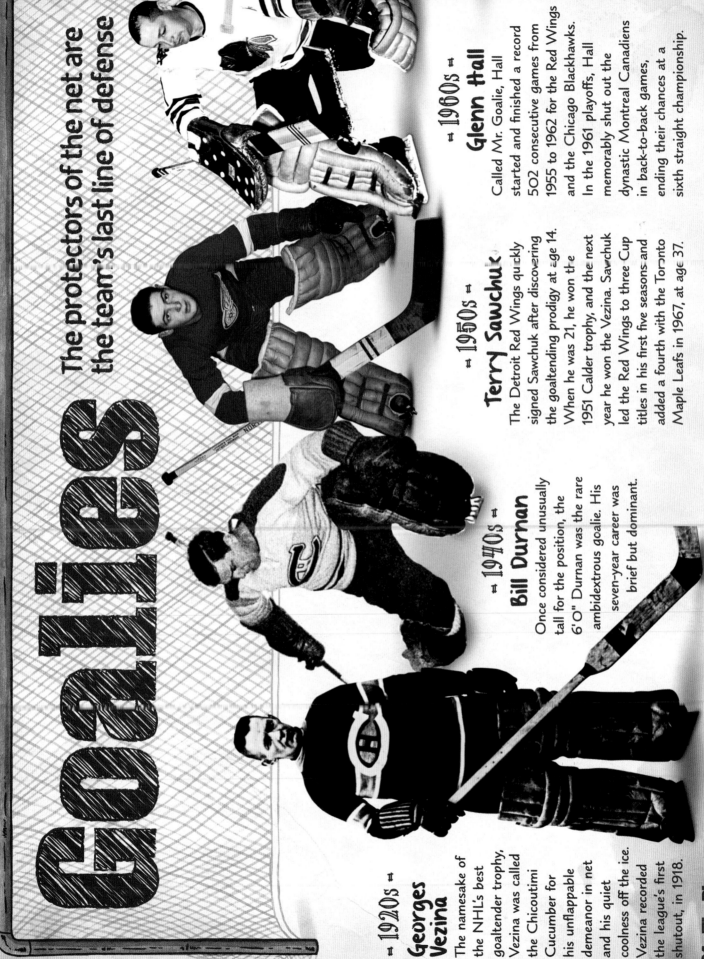

Goalies

The protectors of the net are the team's last line of defense

= 1920s =
Georges Vezina

The namesake of the NHL's best goaltender trophy, Vezina was called the Chicoutimi Cucumber for his unflappable demeanor in net and his quiet coolness off the ice. Vezina recorded the league's first shutout, 1918.

= 1940s =
Bill Durnan

Once considered unusually tall for the position, the 6'0" Durnan was the rare ambidextrous goalie. His seven-year career was brief but dominant.

= 1950s =
Terry Sawchuk

The Detroit Red Wings quickly signed Sawchuk after discovering the goaltending prodigy at age 14. When he was 21, he won the 1951 Calder trophy, and the next year he won the Vezina. Sawchuk led the Red Wings to three Cup titles in his first five seasons and added a fourth with the Toronto Maple Leafs in 1967, at age 37.

= 1960s =
Glenn Hall

Called Mr. Goalie, Hall started and finished a record 502 consecutive games from 1955 to 1962 for the Red Wings and the Chicago Blackhawks. In the 1961 playoffs, Hall memorably shut out the dynastic Montreal Canadiens in back-to-back games, ending their chances at a sixth straight championship.

▪ 1970s ▪
Ken Dryden

You could say Dryden's career got off to a unique start; in 1971, he won the Stanley Cup and the Conn Smythe, as playoff MVP, before his rookie season. The Canadiens' netminder was no one-hit wonder, however. He led his team to five more championships.

▪ 1980s ▪
Patrick Roy

The fiery Roy is perhaps best remembered for his postseason dominance with the Colorado Avalanche during the 1990s. But before he lifted a Stanley Cup in Colorado, he won three Vezina Trophies and two Cups with Montreal.

▪ 1990s ▪
Dominik Hasek

During his prime, the Dominator was statistically the best player to stand between the pipes. From 1993–1994 to 1998–1999, Hasek put up a season save percentage of at least .930 five times. Famous for making flailing, unconventional saves, Hasek is the only goalie to win two Hart Trophies as league MVP.

▪ 2000s ▪
Martin Brodeur

Combining excellence with longevity, the longtime Devils netminder retired in 2015 as the all-time leader in wins (691) and shutouts (125). Known for his puckhandling ability, he even inspired a rule that prevented goalies from handling the puck outside a trapezoid area behind the net.

Two-Way for Four

1970s

Bobby Clarke

Nobody worked harder than Clarke, and his exceptional two-way play was the result of his effort. The Philadelphia Flyers' captain would do just about anything to stop an opposing player, whether that was relentlessly checking or fighting. Clarke was the league MVP three times and won the Selke Trophy as the league's best defensive forward in 1982–1983 at age 33. He probably would have won it more often if the award had existed before 1977–1978.

1950s

Marty Pavelich

Pavelich won four Stanley Cups with the Detroit Red Wings, playing with legends such as Gordie Howe and Ted Lindsay. Three of those championships came against the Montreal Canadiens, and Pavelich had perhaps the most important job: covering Habs star Maurice (Rocket) Richard. During the 1954 playoffs, Richard scored just three points in 11 games as the Wings won in the finals in seven games. Pavelich reached a double-digit goal total in four of his 10 NHL seasons.

ards

1990s

It is said that offense comes from great defense, and these players were the best of both worlds

Sergei Fedorov

The epitome of a two-way forward, Fedorov was able to dominate opponents all over the ice. As the linchpin of Detroit's Russian Five, he led the Red Wings to three Stanley Cup championships during the 1990s and early 2000s. In 1993–1994, Fedorov became the only player in NHL history to win both the Hart and Selke trophies in the same year. He finished that season with 56 goals, 64 assists, and a +48 rating.

2010s

Patrice Bergeron

For five consecutive seasons from 2011 through 2016, the Boston Bruins center finished in the top two in Selke Trophy voting and won it three times. During that span, Bergeron led all forwards in face-off winning percentage with 59.1% and was third among forwards with a +112 rating. Defense is just part of Bergeron's value. He also led the Bruins in points during that period, scoring 281 in 364 games.

THEN

Bobby Orr

CAREER	1966–1979
HEIGHT, WEIGHT	6'0", 197 pounds
STYLE	Orr used his unrivaled speed to carry the puck coast-to-coast, from his defensive zone right to the opponent's net.
CAREER HIGHLIGHTS	Orr won the Calder Trophy as the league's best rookie in 1967 and two Norris Trophies as the league's best defenseman before he even turned 21. From 1969–1975, Orr led the league in assists five times, won three Hart Trophies as league MVP, won six more Norris Trophies, and led the Boston Bruins to Stanley Cup victories in 1970 and 1972.
BEST SEASON	1970–1971: 37 goals, 102 assists, 139 points, 91 penalty minutes, +124 rating in 78 games
FUN FACT	The Bobby Orr Hall of Fame is a museum dedicated almost entirely to the Hall of Famer, located in his hometown of Parry Sound, Ontario.
QUOTABLE	"It felt like a five-player stampede moving toward you—and at his pace. He pushed his teammates [because] you're playing with the best player in the league." —Ken Dryden

These blueliners changed the way the

offensive D

defensemen

position was played in his era

Erik Karlsson

CAREER	2009–present
HEIGHT, WEIGHT	6'0", 191 pounds
STYLE	With stick skills as good as any forward's, Karlsson dangles past defenders and finds teammates with crisp passes.
CAREER HIGHLIGHTS	Karlsson scored 78 points in 2011–2012 and became a surprise Norris Trophy winner that year at age 21. From 2011 to the present, Karlsson has led all defensemen with 385 points in 421 games. In 2015–2016, the Ottawa Senator became the first blueliner to lead the league in assists since . . . Bobby Orr.
BEST SEASON	2011–2012: 19 goals, 59 assists, 78 points, 42 penalty minutes, +16 rating in 81 games
FUN FACT	When the Senators took Karlsson 15th at the 2008 draft in Ottawa, fellow Swede Daniel Alfredsson announced the pick.
QUOTABLE	"There are probably some coaches who wouldn't let him go like he does. They let me go. I couldn't imagine playing any other way, and I can't imagine young Erik playing any other way, either." —Bobby Orr

Fighters

Punches have been in hockey nearly as long as pucks. And even though the role of fighting in the game has **decreased over time,** these three classes of combatants have **remained**

★ THEN ★
KEN LINSEMAN

Nicknamed the Rat, Linseman had a knack for annoying opposing players. The 5'11" center had a well-deserved reputation for cheap shots and other dirty plays. Like many of the pests who followed in his footsteps, Linseman did not seek out fights, but he found himself in a fair number of them anyway as a result of his antics. Along with 807 points, he had 1,727 career penalty minutes.

★ NOW ★
ANTOINE ROUSSEL

In the modern NHL, teams don't have the luxury of keeping a slow, hulking enforcer who doesn't have much value offensively. Pests like Roussel, however, can actually help with offense. They draw penalties that put their teams on the power play. In 2015–2016, Roussel fought nine times, but he also drew 36 penalties and scored 13 goals.

TOUGH GUYS

ENFORCERS

★ THEN ★ — TED LINDSAY

Terrible Ted was not to be taken lightly as a scorer or as a fighting partner. Playing with Gordie Howe, Lindsay provided Detroit's Production Line with grit. At the time of his retirement, Lindsay was the NHL's all-time leader in penalty minutes with 1,808. But he was also third all-time in points with 851.

★ NOW ★ — MILAN LUCIC

Lucic typifies the modern power forward: an imposing figure who uses his size to create space around the net and intimidate opponents. The 6'3" winger has gotten into 64 fights and scored 182 goals in 10 seasons. The Oilers signed Lucic to a seven-year contract in 2016, in part to protect their young stars.

★ THEN ★ — DAVE SCHULTZ

With players like gritty captain Bobby Clarke and Linseman, the Philadelphia Flyers of the 1970s earned the nickname the Broad Street Bullies. And Dave (the Hammer) Schultz was the biggest bully of them all. His 472 penalty minutes in 1974–1975 is the most ever in a single season.

★ NOW ★ — JARED BOLL

Just five years ago, the 6'3", 209-pound Boll had to worry about facing fellow heavyweights like Donald Brashear (6'2", 235 lbs.) and Jody Shelley (6'3", 225 lbs.). These days, however, the game has become less violent. In 2016–2017, Boll averaged just 1:42 in the penalty box per game.

Characters

From a goalie obsessed with the moon to a defenseman called the Planet, these are the most colorful individuals to ever play the sport

≈ 1970s ≈

Gilles Gratton

As a group, goaltenders have a reputation for being a little off, and Gratton is one reason why. Beyond his infamous tiger mask, Grattoony the Loony once refused to play because of where the moon was in the sky.

≈ 1960s ≈

Eddie Shack

Yet another colorful Maple Leaf, Shack had two self-explanatory nicknames: the Nose and the Entertainer. The mustached winger even inspired a 1966 number 1 hit single by Douglas Rankine with The Secrets: "Clear the Track, Here Comes Eddie Shack."

≈ 1940s ≈

Turk Broda

One of the league's first media darlings, the Toronto goalie once said, "The Leafs pay me for my work in practices, and I throw games in for free." He also had a sense of humor about his weight, which he and coach Conn Smythe fought over in the "Battle of the Bulge."

≈ 1930s ≈

Eddie Shore

The legendary Toronto Maple Leafs defenseman seemed to get stranger with age. As an owner and coach, Shore would make his players tap-dance, believing it would improve their balance. He also wrestled them in an attempt to adjust their spines.

Tiger Williams

≡ 1980s ≡

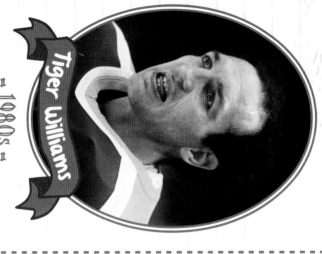

The NHL's all-time leader in penalty minutes with 3,966, Williams must have been saying something to start all those fights. The witty winger always had a clever retort in interviews and famously rode his stick like a witch's broom after one goal.

Al Iafrate

≡ 1990s ≡

Iafrate may have seemed a little out of place in hockey, but he was at home in the 1990s. Balding but still sporting a mullet, Iafrate loved heavy metal music, motorcycles, and tattoos. One sportswriter took to calling Iafrate the Planet because he was so out there.

Ilya Bryzgalov

≡ 2000s ≡

Speaking of planets, how about former goaltender Bryzgalov, who went viral when he discussed cosmology on HBO's 24/7 in 2011? Whether discussing the stars or his fear of bears, Bryz provided plenty of good sound bites.

Brent Burns

≡ 2010s ≡

While some people are said to wear their personalities on their sleeve, Burns wears it on his face with his shaggy beard and toothless grin. An avid animal lover, the Sharks' defenseman frequently visits zoos on road trips, and he even used to breed snakes in his home.

Player size

Hockey has always welcomed players of all heights—proving bigger isn't always better on ice

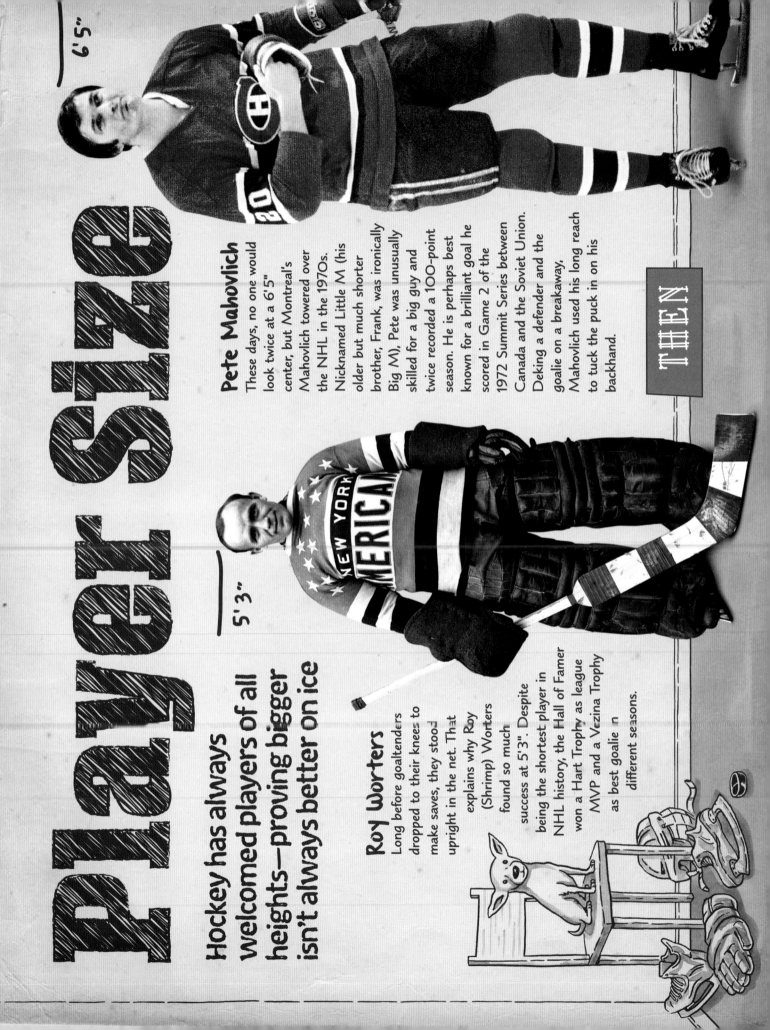

6'5"

5'3"

Pete Mahovlich

These days, no one would look twice at a 6'5" center, but Montreal's Mahovlich towered over the NHL in the 1970s. Nicknamed Little M (his older but much shorter brother, Frank, was ironically Big M). Pete was unusually skilled for a big guy and twice recorded a 100-point season. He is perhaps best known for a brilliant goal he scored in Game 2 of the 1972 Summit Series between Canada and the Soviet Union. Deking a defender and the goalie on a breakaway, Mahovlich used his long reach to tuck the puck in on his backhand.

Roy Worters

Long before goaltenders dropped to their knees to make saves, they stood upright in the net. That explains why Roy (Shrimp) Worters found so much success at 5'3". Despite being the shortest player in NHL history, the Hall of Famer won a Hart Trophy as league MVP and a Vezina Trophy as best goalie in different seasons.

Brian Gionta

It's a testament to how much taller NHLers are now that the 5'7" Gionta is among the league's very shortest players. Five-foot-five Nathan Gerbe, who played for the Sabres, is now in Europe, while 5'6" forwards Joe Whitney and Rocco Grimaldi are both in the minors. That leaves Brian and his brother Stephen, also 5'7", literally looking up to the rest of the league, but maybe not for long. A new generation of shorter skilled players, such as Calgary Flames winger Johnny Gaudreau (5'9"), are starting to gain more respect.

5'7"

NOW

Zdeno Chara

Even as a defenseman—a position suited for tall players—Chara towers over his peers. The Bruins' captain stands 7-feet tall on his skates, so the league allows him to use a 65-inch stick, two inches longer than regulation. In other words, if his stick blade were bent straight, the entire thing would be two inches taller than Worters! That long reach helps explain why he is one of the league's best pokecheckers. His extra long shaft also handles enough force to produce the NHL's hardest slap shot, measured at a record 108.8 mph.

6'9"

careers

Hockey players are known for having long careers, which has led to surprising generational overlap

Wayne Gretzky and Gordie Howe may be the two greatest hockey players of all time. They first met when Gretzky was 10 or so. Howe had just wrapped up a legendary 25-year career with the Detroit Red Wings. Howe, known simply as Mr. Hockey, was in Brantford, Ontario for a banquet. Gretzky, a Brantford native, had his picture taken with his idol hooking him around the neck (below). Looking at this famous photo, it seems impossible to think the two would one day play against each other.

They did, though, first in the upstart World Hockey Association, and then for one season in the NHL when Howe was 51 and Gretzky was 19. Several hockey players have had extreme longevity. This has created other notable overlapping careers. Use this time line to chart the careers of your favorites today and the stars of yesterday.

Though they dominated different decades, Howe and Gretzky both played in the World Hockey Association in 1978–1979. When the WHA merged with the NHL the next season, Howe's last year in the league would be Gretzky's first.

Gordie Howe
1946–1971, 1973–1980

Maurice Richard
1942–1969

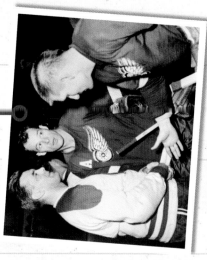

Montreal's Rocket Richard (left) was the preeminent goal scorer of the 1940s and an early rival of Howe (center).

Henri Richard
1955–1975

1940   1945   1950   1955   1960   1965

Wayne Gretzky
1978–1999

Guy Lafleur
1971–1991

Peter Stastny
1980–1995

Mario Lemieux
1984–1997, 2000–2006

Joe Sakic
1988–2009

Sidney Crosby
2005–present

Paul Stastny
2006–present

Guy Lafleur (left) led the Canadiens to a dynasty in the 1970s and finished his career with the Quebec Nordiques, playing along young star Joe Sakic (right).

Maric Lemieux (right) had a brilliant career from 1984 to 1997 with the Pittsburgh Penguins. Then, as the team's owner, he came out of retirement and played five more seasons, including one with Sidney Crosby (left).

Sakic (left) started his career in Quebec, where he was teammates with Peter Stastny. Then the Nordiques moved to Colorado, where Sakic would eventually play with Peter's son Paul (right) for three seasons.

From coaching strategies to growing participation abroad, hockey is much more than just sticks and pucks. To truly understand the spirit of hockey, you have to look beyond the NHL's biggest stars.

Hockey is, after all, the ultimate team sport. So how do you get a group of skaters to play like a team—and win consistently to become a dynasty? That's the big question and the game's ultimate goal.

Coaches

These bench bosses are the best of the best and have won 38 Stanley Cups combined

1950s

Toe Blake

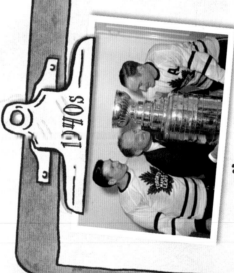

Blake had an outstanding playing career, winning three Stanley Cups and one Hart Trophy as league MVP with the Montreal Canadiens in the 1930s and 1940s. But it was behind the Montreal bench where Blake did his best work. His Habs teams won the Stanley Cup in each of his first five seasons as coach and then three more times after that.

1960s

Punch Imlach

Originally a member of the Maple Leafs' front office, Imlach took over as coach in the middle of the 1958–1959 season. Even though he never played in the NHL himself, Imlach engineered his team's miraculous comeback that season and helped the Leafs earn a playoff berth. Then, starting in 1961–1962, he coached the team to three straight Cups and a fourth in 1966–1967. The Maple Leafs haven't won another championship since. Imlach's 365 wins remains a franchise record.

1940s

Hap Day

His leadership qualities made Day the Toronto Maple Leafs' first captain, an honor he held for a decade. So it was no surprise that the Leafs were eager to hire him to coach once his playing days were over. The move paid off almost immediately. In his second season behind the bench, Day led the Leafs to a historic comeback, defeating the Red Wings in the Cup finals after being down three games to none.

1930s

Jack Adams

The first general manager and coach of the Detroit Cougars (who became the Red Wings in 1932), Adams was the architect that built Motor City into one of hockey's great markets. As a manager, he expertly used scouting and minor league farm teams to nurture the Wings' Hall of Fame core. As a coach, he was fiery toward opponents (and often referees) but caring to his own players. A winner of three Stanley Cups with Detroit, he is the namesake of the NHL's annual award for best coach.

Scotty Bowman

Arguably the greatest bench boss of all time, Bowman is the only coach to win the Stanley Cup with three franchises—and in three decades. His first five rings came in the 1970s with Montreal, where he coached for eight seasons. He then won his sixth in 1992 with the Pittsburgh Penguins and superstar Mario Lemieux, before finishing his career in Detroit, where he won three more Cups as a coach—an NHL record.

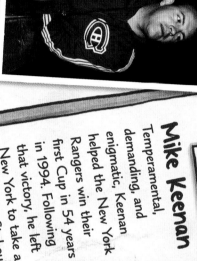

1970s

Al Arbour

A defenseman on two of Punch Imlach's championship teams, Arbour would become a coaching legend himself, leading the New York Islanders to four straight Stanley Cups in the 1980s. After coaching 1,499 games over 19 seasons with New York, Arbour unretired on a one-game contract in 2007 to guide the Islanders to a 3–2 win over the Pittsburgh Penguins, giving him an even 1,500 with the franchise.

1980s

Mike Keenan

Temperamental, demanding, and enigmatic, Keenan helped the New York Rangers win their first Cup in 54 years in 1994. Following that victory, he left New York to take a job with the St. Louis Blues, but he only lasted there for three seasons. He never kept jobs for very long, but he was almost always successful. In his career, he has also won an AHL title, a Canadian collegiate championship, and most recently a KHL championship in Russia.

1990s

Mike Babcock

Babcock's Detroit Red Wings excelled in the second half of the 2000s, playing a puck-possession style that the rest of the league would come to emulate. After coaching Team Canada to two Olympic golds, Babcock signed an eight-year, $50 million contract with the Maple Leafs in 2015, becoming the highest-paid coach in NHL history.

2000s

Joel Quenneville

Under Quenneville, the Blackhawks have won three Cups in their last nine seasons, an impressive accomplishment in today's salary cap era. Quenneville had also previously won the Jack Adams Award as best coach for the 1999–2000 season, when his St. Louis Blues finished with the best record in the NHL.

2010s

Strategies

OFFENSE

Stay in Lane

Before players realized the importance of puck possession and the power of creative passing, skaters rarely veered from their lanes on the ice. The right wing and right defenseman stayed to the right, the left wing and left defenseman stayed left, and the center kept to the middle. They did not have much choice—the original rules regarding passing were restrictive and encouraged players to skate straight ahead and shoot. Defensemen were less likely to pinch in the offensive zone.

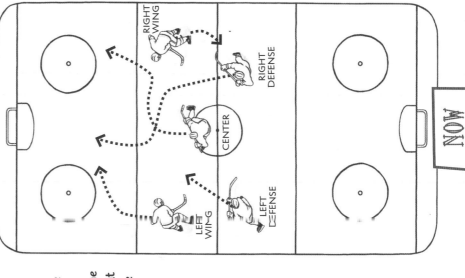

Crisscross

The 1972 Summit Series between Canada and the Soviet Union changed hockey tactics forever. The Canadians, assuming that all the best players in the world were in the NHL, expected to win easily. They were shocked when the Soviet team won the first game 7–3, skating circles around their Canadian counterparts. The Soviet forwards weaved left and right, while the defensemen rushed through the neutral zone—a model for future NHL teams.

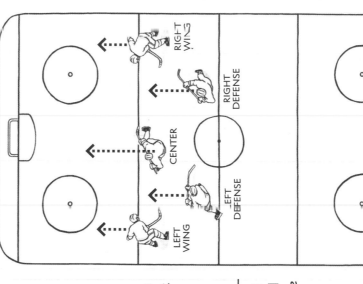

THEN

NOW

Whether on the forecheck, the backcheck, offense, or defense, on-ice tactics have evolved from rudimentary to very complex

DEFENSE

Left Wing Lock

Used to great effect by the Detroit Red Wings in the 1990s, the left wing lock (or weak side lock) involves one forward—often, but not always the left wing—dropping back and playing alongside the two defensemen to defend the blue line. The other two forwards may then pressure the puck-carrier, trying to force a turnover. The system is designed to prevent odd-man rushes, as the defending team always has at least three skaters back.

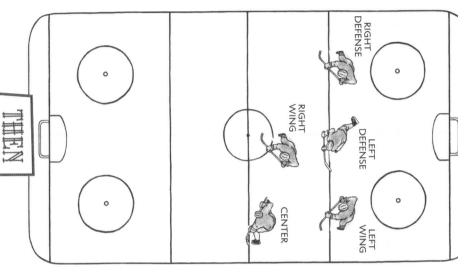

THEN

One-Three-One

So-called neutral zone traps fell out of favor after the NHL changed the rules in 2005, allowing a two-line pass in the neutral zone. In the 2011–2012 season, the Tampa Bay Lightning attempted to revive something similar under coach Guy Boucher. One forward pressures the puck-carrier as he exits the zone, while a defenseman and two forwards stand astride in the neutral zone to cover an outlet pass. The other defenseman stays back to play safety.

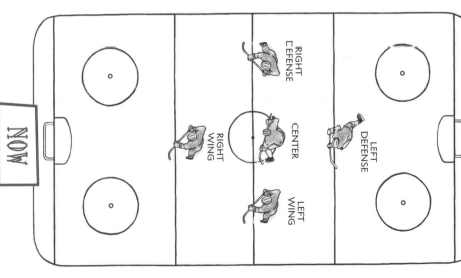

NOW

Global Games

1920–1992

W inning international sporting competitions can build up pride in any nation, but it was especially emphasized in the Union of Soviet Socialist Republics, where the government identified athletes at a young age to compete for their country. The Soviet men's hockey team lived and practiced together nearly year-round so that the players could improve their chemistry for the Olympics and world championships.

It worked. Until the 1960s, Canada predictably dominated the sport it had created.

But from 1963 to 1990, the U.S.S.R. won an astounding 20 out of 25 IIHF World Championships and six of seven Olympic gold medal games. It was not always facing the world's best players, however, because the NHL didn't allow its players to compete at the Winter Games before 1998.

Vladislav Tretiak, Team USSR

39 Medals — U.S.S.R.

38 Medals — Czechoslovakia

37 Medals — Canada

16 Medals — United States

Check out how different the international hockey landscape looked before, during, and after the Cold War

1993–Present

Three events in the 1990s shifted power in the international hockey scene. First, in 1991 the Cold War ended and the Soviet Union dissolved, breaking up hockey's preeminent force. Second, women's hockey arrived on the scene. In 1990, the IIHF held its first Women's World Championships, and then in 1998, a women's tournament was added to the Nagano Winter Olympics. And finally, also in 1998, the NHL allowed its players to participate in the Olympics. Since then, Team Canada—both the men and women—have been dominant. In the men's game, Sweden has emerged as a worthy challenger, winning Olympic gold in 2006. Meanwhile, the Canadian women have built a spirited rivalry against the United States. With the NHL's decision to withdraw from the 2018 Games, however, Canada's chances at an Olympic men's three-peat may be threatened.

Carey Price,
Team Canada

Sweden **23 Medals**

United States **29 Medals**

Finland **31 Medals**

Canada **39 Medals**

Units

These fearsome groups of five propelled their home countries to international success

=THEN=

The Soviet Union's national hockey team was the world's most intimidating for much of the 1980s, in large part because of the unstoppable team play of their starting five: *(from left)* defenseman Alexei Kasatonov, right wing Sergei Makarov, center Igor Larionov, left wing Vladimir Krutov, and defenseman-captain Slava Fetisov. Known as the Green Unit for the color of the jerseys they wore during team practices, these five players were so in sync on the ice that it almost seemed as if their moves were choreographed. Together, they won Olympic gold medals in 1984 and 1988. They all eventually pursued NHL careers, and Larionov and Fetisov went on to win the Stanley Cup with the Detroit Red Wings.

= NOW =

While they don't practice together all year like the Soviet national team did, Canada's best players have led their country on quite a run of recent international successes, winning Olympic gold medals in 2010 and 2014 and the 2016 World Cup of Hockey. Team Canada's top forward line and defense pairing for the World Cup were stacked with the NHL's best two-way players: *(from left)* right wing Patrice Bergeron, left wing Brad Marchand, center Sidney Crosby, defenseman Shea Weber, and defenseman Marc-Édouard Vlasic. Crosby, Marchand, and Bergeron were the tournament's three top-scoring forwards, while the defensemen were a combined +7 through 11 games.

Records

To understand Wayne Gretzky's incredible accomplishments and his enduring legacy, just take a look at the numbers

GOALS IN A SEASON

1. Phil Esposito 76 1970–1971
2. Mike Bossy 69 1978–1979
3. Phil Esposito 68 1973–1974
4. Phil Esposito 66 1971–1972
5. Phil Esposito 61 1974–1975
5. Reggie Leach 61 1975–1976
7. Steve Shutt 60 1976–1977
7. Guy Lafleur 60 1977–1978
9. Steve Shutt 59 1978–1979
9. Marcel Dionne 59 1978–1979

POINTS IN A SEASON

1. Phil Esposito 152 1970–1971
2. Phil Esposito 145 1973–1974
3. Bobby Orr 139 1970–1971

4. Guy Lafleur 136 1976–1977
5. Bobby Orr 135 1974–1975
6. Bryan Trottier .. 134 1978–1979
7. Phil Esposito ... 133 1971–1972
8. Guy Lafleur 132 1977–1978
9. Phil Esposito ... 130 1972–1973
9. Marcel Dionne... 130 1978–1979

CAREER GOALS

1. Gordie Howe 786
2. Phil Esposito 676
3. Bobby Hull 604
4. John Bucyk 556
5. Maurice Richard 544
6. Stan Mikita 539
7. Frank Mahovlich 533

8. Jean Béliveau 507
9. Norm Ullman 490
10. Alex Delvecchio 456

CAREER POINTS

1. Gordie Howe 1,809
2. Phil Esposito 1,492
3. Stan Mikita 1,460
4. John Bucyk 1,369
5. Alex Delvecchio 1,281
6. Norm Ullman 1,229
7. Jean Béliveau 1,219
8. Jean Ratelle 1,157
9. Bobby Hull 1,153
10. Frank Mahovlich ... 1,103

GOALS IN A SEASON

1. Wayne Gretzky	92	1981–1982
2. Wayne Gretzky	87	1983–1984
3. Brett Hull	86	1990–1991
4. Mario Lemieux	85	1988–1989
5. Phil Esposito	76	1970–1971
5. Alexander Mogilny	76	1992–1993
5. Teemu Selanne	76	1992–1993
8. Wayne Gretzky	73	1984–1985
9. Brett Hull	72	1989–1990
10. Wayne Gretzky	71	1982–1983
10. Jari Kurri	71	1984–1985

POINTS IN A SEASON

1. Wayne Gretzky	215	1985–1986
2. Wayne Gretzky	212	1981–1982
3. Wayne Gretzky	208	1984–1985
4. Wayne Gretzky	205	1983–1984
5. Mario Lemieux	199	1988–1989
6. Wayne Gretzky	196	1982–1983
7. Wayne Gretzky	183	1987–1988
8. Mario Lemieux	168	1987–1988
8. Wayne Gretzky	168	1988–1989
10. Wayne Gretzky	164	1980–1981

CAREER GOALS

1. Wayne Gretzky	894
2. Gordie Howe	801
3. Jaromir Jagr	765
4. Brett Hull	741
5. Marcel Dionne	731
6. Phil Esposito	717
7. Mike Gartner	708
8. Mark Messier	694
9. Steve Yzerman	692
10. Mario Lemieux	690

CAREER POINTS

1. Wayne Gretzky	2,857
2. Jaromir Jagr	1,914
3. Mark Messier	1,887
4. Gordie Howe	1,850
5. Ron Francis	1,798
6. Marcel Dionne	1,771
7. Steve Yzerman	1,755
8. Mario Lemieux	1,723
9. Joe Sakic	1,641
10. Phil Esposito	1,590

Wayne Gretzky
It seems unlikely that another player will ever approach—much less break—the Great One's record of 2,857 career NHL points.

Women's Hockey

These female trailblazers have proved over the years that hockey is a game for everyone

= 1930s =
Hilda Ranscombe

Originally a softball team that went on to play hockey in the winter months, the Preston Rivulettes dominated the Ladies Ontario Hockey Association, losing just two games out of 350 during the decade. Ranscombe was the team's captain and best player. Noted for her speed, she was considered the best female hockey player in the world at the time.

HILDA

= 1920s =
Bobbie Rosenfeld

Once called the superwoman of ladies' hockey, Rosenfeld was in fact a superb all-around athlete. On the ice, she won championships with the Toronto Patterson Pats in the North Toronto Ladies' City League. She also took home a gold in the 4x100 relay and a silver in the 100-yard dash for Canada at the 1928 Olympics.

= 1950s =
Abby Hoffman

With no girls' leagues to join, nine-year-old Abby Hoffman cut her hair and registered in a boys' league as Ab Hoffman. Her success was her undoing, however, as making an All-Star team forced her to show her birth certificate. Like Rosenfeld, she eventually grew up to be a track and field Olympian.

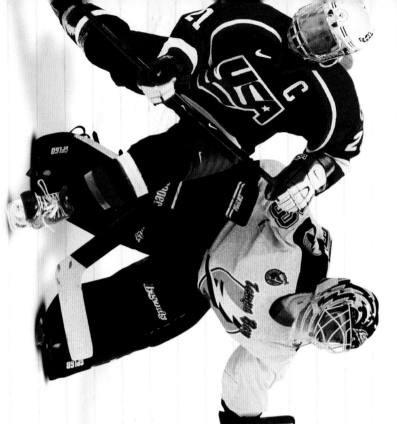

Cammi Granato

═ 1990s ═

While starring for Providence College in the early 1990s, Granato became part of the first U.S. women's national team in 1990. Eight years later she captained the U.S. to gold at the first Olympic women's hockey tournament in Nagano, Japan. She would retire with 115 points in 64 international games. In 2010, Granato and Canada's Angela James became the first women inducted, as players, into the Hockey Hall of Fame.

Manon Rhéaume

On September 23, 1992, Rhéaume made history when she played goalie for the Tampa Bay Lightning in a preseason game, making her the first woman to play in an official NHL-sanctioned contest. She stopped seven of nine shots and left the game after the first period. Rhéaume went on to play for six other men's pro teams in the IHL and the ECHL.

Hayley Wickenheiser

═ 2000s ═

A-guably the greatest women's hockey player of all time, Wickenheiser joined Team Canada at age 15 ard would go on to win four straight Olympic gold medals, including one as captain. In 2003, she became the first woman to score a goal in a professional men's game, as a member of HC Salamat in Finland.

Hilary Knight

═ 2010s ═

After becoming the first American to be MVP of the Canadian Women's Hockey League, in 2012-2013, Knight went or to lead the National Women's Hockey League in points during its inaugural season three years later. Her team, the Boston Pride, won the first league championship. As an international star, she has led the U.S. to two Olympic silver medals and seven World Championship golds.

Goals

Nothing in the game is more thrilling than a spectacular one-man effort that leads to a score

≡ 1988 ≡
Denis Savard

In the winter of 1988, the Edmonton Oilers were on their way to winning their fourth Stanley Cup in five seasons. That only made it more amazing when, on February 24, Chicago's Savard beat five different Oilers, including goalie Grant Fuhr, to score an unforgettable shorthanded goal. On arguably the best man-down shift in NHL history, the Blackhawks' center made three future Hall of Famers look silly.

≡ 1991 ≡
Mario Lemieux

With his Pittsburgh Penguins trailing the Minnesota North Stars by one game in the 1991 Stanley Cup finals, Lemieux stepped up in Game 2, scoring perhaps the most memorable goal in Cup finals history. Lemieux went end-to-end in the second period, skating between both Minnesota defensemen, and collided with goaltender Jon Casey just as he scored on a backhanded shot that gave Pittsburgh a 3–1 lead.

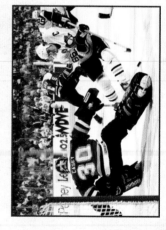

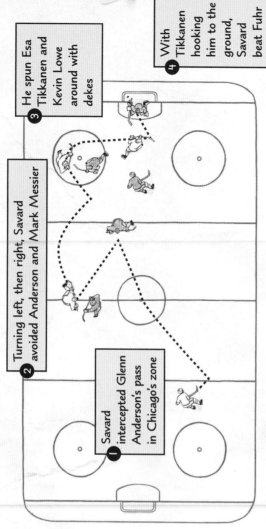

1 Savard intercepted Glenn Anderson's pass in Chicago's zone

2 Turning left, then right, Savard avoided Anderson and Mark Messier

3 He spun Esa Tikkanen and Kevin Lowe around with dekes

4 With Tikkanen hooking him to the ground, Savard beat Fuhr

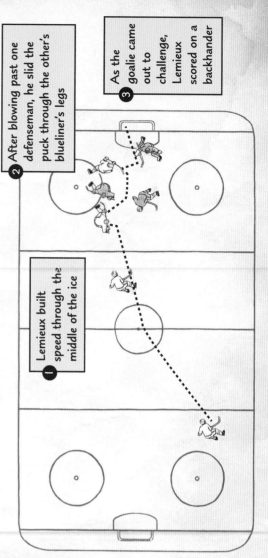

1 Lemieux built speed through the middle of the ice

2 After blowing past one defenseman, he slid the puck through the other's blueliner's legs

3 As the goalie came out to challenge, Lemieux scored on a backhander

≈ 2003 ≈
Peter Forsberg

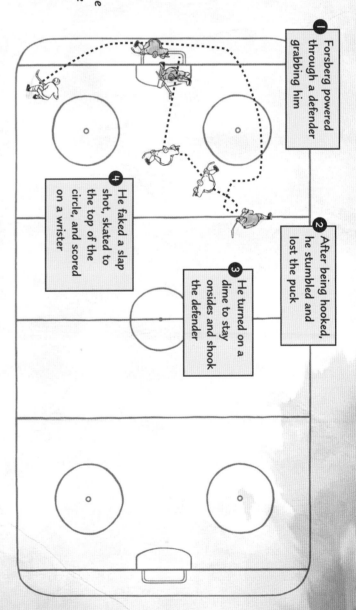

On February 9, 2003, the Colorado Avalanche center scored a hat trick against the Calgary Flames, though his second and third goals were no match for his first of the evening. Midway through the opening period, with a defender draped all over him, Forsberg somehow kept possession of the puck as he skated behind the net. Retreating toward the blue line, he was hooked, stumbled, and lost the puck. But all in one motion he recovered it, deked a defender, and cut to the net, scoring high blocker-side on Flames goalie Roman Turek.

1 Forsberg powered through a defender grabbing him

2 After being hooked, he stumbled and lost the puck

3 He turned on a dime to stay onsides and shook the defender

4 He faked a slap shot, skated to the top of the circle, and scored on a wrister

≈ 2006 ≈
Alexander Ovechkin

Despite scoring 558 times so far in his 12-year career, Ovechkin has yet to top a goal from his rookie season. In an otherwise meaningless game between the Phoenix Coyotes and the Washington Capitals, two basement-dwelling teams, Ovechkin streaked into the zone one-on-one against Phoenix defenseman Paul Mara. After a failed toe-drag left him flat on his back, Ovechkin scored by swooping the puck—with only one hand on his stick—to the back of the net. Even the Coyotes' coach at the time, Wayne Gretzky, was impressed with what has become known as the Goal.

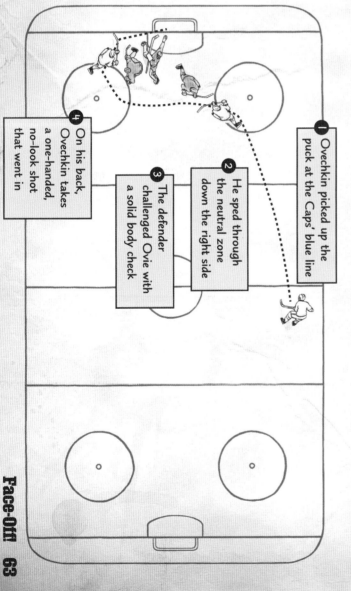

1 Ovechkin picked up the puck at the Caps' blue line

2 He sped through the neutral zone down the right side

3 The defender challenged Ovie with a solid body check

4 On his back, Ovechkin takes a one-handed, no-look shot that went in

Dynasties

Montreal Canadiens
1955–1960

With 24 Stanley Cup victories (the most of any team by a margin of 11), the Canadiens could rightly describe many eras in their history as dynastic. The franchise's greatest accomplishment, however, is winning five Cups in a row from 1956 to 1960. With brothers Henri and Maurice Richard leading the offense and Vezina-winning goalie Jacques Plante in net, the Habs dominated on both sides of the puck.

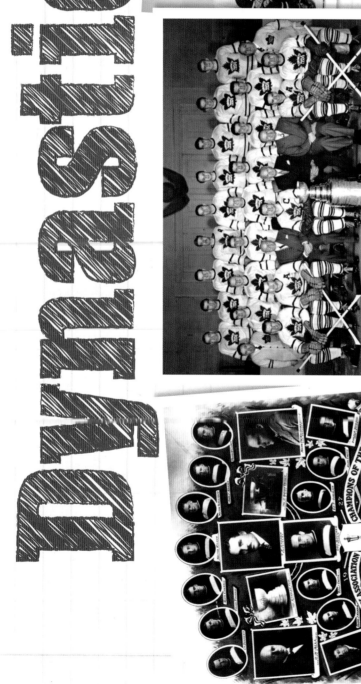

Toronto Maple Leafs
1941–1951

Despite their modest accomplishments in the modern era, the Leafs had two great dynasties, the first of which was led by captain Syl Apps in the 1940s. After losing six out of eight Stanley Cup finals in the previous decade, coach Hap Day led the Leafs to five championships in eight seasons, starting in 1941. His successor, Joe Primeau, would add a sixth in 1951.

Ottawa Senators
1918–1927

Not the same franchise as today's Ottawa Senators, which only joined the NHL in 1992, these original Sens were the NHL's first dynasty. In 16 seasons they appeared in seven finals and won four league championships. Stacked with future Hall of Famers like Frank Nighbor and King Clancy, the Senators, also known as the Silver Seven, had won seven Stanley Cup titles before the NHL was even formed.

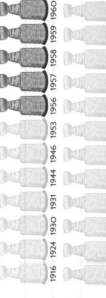

| 1916 | 1924 | 1930 | 1931 | 1944 | 1946 | 1953 | 1956 | 1957 | 1958 | 1959 | 1960 |
| 1965 | 1966 | 1968 | 1969 | 1971 | 1973 | 1976 | 1977 | 1978 | 1979 | 1986 | 1993 |

| 1918 | 1922 | 1932 | 1942 | 1945 | 1947 | 1948 | 1949 | 1951 | 1962 | 1963 | 1964 | 1967 |

| 1903 | 1904 | 1905 | 1906 | 1909 | 1910 | 1911 | 1920 | 1921 | 1921 | 1923 | 1927 |

From Ottawa's Super Six to the Islanders' Drive for Five, these teams made winning championships look easy

1979–1983

New York Islanders

After entering the league in 1972, the Islanders drafted well, quickly accumulating elite players at every position. By their fourth season, New York had its first 100-point finish. And four years after that, they won the first of four straight Stanley Cups. Linemates Mike Bossy and Bryan Trottier gave the Isles an offense that could challenge Wayne Gretzky's Oilers, while the team's grit went unmatched. Their Drive for Five was cut short in 1984, when a new dynasty took off.

1980 1981 1982 1983

1984–1990

Edmonton Oilers

After years of chasing the Islanders, Edmonton finally broke through in 1984. With Gretzky in his prime, the Oilers couldn't help but have the league's best offense. During their first Cup-winning season, the Oilers scored 446 regular-season goals. The next best offense in their conference had just 345 and allowed 30 more goals on defense! After Gretzky was traded to the Los Angeles Kings in 1988, Edmonton, led by Mark Messier, would win a fifth in 1990.

1984 1985 1987 1988 1990

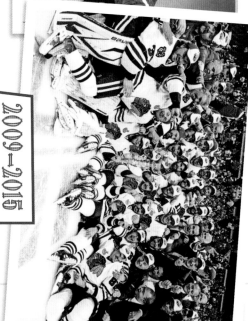

2009–2015

Chicago Blackhawks

In the modern NHL, where teams must stay under a salary cap, dynasties are harder to come by. But the Blackhawks did the improbable by winning three championships in six seasons. The first, in 2010, broke the franchise's 49-year Stanley Cup drought. Led by center Jonathan Toews (who Chicago took third in the 2006 draft) and winger Patrick Kane (No. 1 in 2007), the Blackhawks have demonstrated the importance of making the most of draft picks in today's NHL.

1934 1938 1961 2010 2013 2015

Stanley Cup

The NHL's iconic trophy is older than the league itself. Chart its evolution from silver bowl to sacred prize

Sir Frederick Arthur Stanley, Lord Stanley of Preston and son of the Earl of Derby, bought the original trophy for 10 guineas (about $50 today) in 1892. Appointed the Governor General of Canada by England's Queen Victoria, Lord Stanley watched his first hockey game at the 1888 Montreal Winter Carnival. He was so impressed by the contest that he decided to donate a prize to be awarded to "the championship hockey club of the Dominion of Canada." The next year the Montreal Amateur Athletic Association won the first Stanley Cup, 24 years before the NHL was established. The Cup has grown in size quite a bit since—and is no longer open to challengers from outside the NHL. Still, it remains hockey's most coveted prize and an enduring symbol of the sport's history.

1893–1914

The original Stanley Cup was really just a cup, or more accurately, a bowl. Engraved with the words FROM STANLEY OF PRESTON, the Cup only changed hands when a challenger defeated the reigning champions. From 1893 to 1914, nine teams had turns as Stanley Cup winners. Ottawa's hockey club was the era's most successful team, holding on to it from 1903 to 1906.

1915–1925

Starting in 1915, the Stanley Cup stopped being awarded through a challenge system and instead went to the winners of a tournament involving Canada's best professional leagues. In 1917, the Seattle Metropolitans became the first American team to take the Cup.

1926–1947

In 1925, nine years into the NHL's existence, the Victoria Cougars became the last non-NHL team to win the Stanley Cup. The following year the league took over the Cup, and it became the championship trophy.

1948–1993

Having players' names engraved into the trophy became a tradition, but before long there was no more room left on the bowl. Equal-sized silver bands were added underneath to commemorate new champions. Eventually this Stovepipe Cup became too unwieldy, so the league designed uneven bands in 1947 and then added the modern wide base in 1958. The original Cup was retired to the Hockey Hall of Fame in Toronto in 1969.

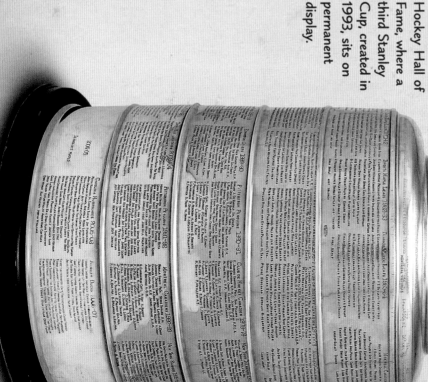

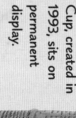

1993–Present

By 1991, all five lower bands of the Stanley Cup were filled with names. To prevent the trophy from growing too large, the league removed the top band and added a new one to the bottom. It has continued this practice ever since, preserving the retired bands at the Hockey Hall of Fame, where a third Stanley Cup, created in 1993, sits on permanent display.

Hockey may not be the world's most popular sport, but its fans rank among the most passionate in the sports world. They love to paint their faces, dress up in wacky costumes, and taunt the other team. That enthusiasm has also led to some unique traditions. Whether growing out a playoff beard along with their team's players or throwing dead fish onto the ice—seriously—hockey lovers will go to zany lengths to prove their loyalty.

Playoff Beards

This postseason superstition is now a time-honored tradition

2006

Mike Commodore wins the award for best hair-and-beard combo. His bushy red locks and coordinating facial hair were a memorable part of the Carolina Hurricanes' first championship.

1995

After the Islanders' dynasty years, the facial hair craze quieted down. But the beard made a comeback with the 1992–1993 Montreal Canadiens and the 1994–1995 New Jersey Devils. "I thought it was a good look for the playoffs: beard and no teeth," Devils defenseman Ken Daneyko *(far right)* told NHL.com.

1989

Calgary Flames right wing Lanny McDonald's trademark bushy mustache got some company in 1989. The Hall of Famer grew a matching beard, as he captained the Flames to their first and still only Stanley Cup.

1980

The New York Islanders were the first to famously put away the razors. Legend has it they were copying tennis star Bjorn Borg *(below)*, who had a habit of growing out his beard during Wimbledon. Islanders players Stefan Persson and Anders Kallur may have borrowed the idea from their Swedish countryman.

Those shaggy Islanders won four straight Stanley Cups and inspired a long-standing tradition.

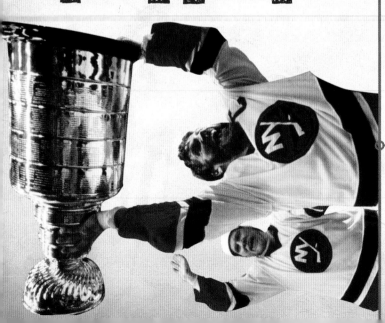

70 Fan Fun

Baby-faced Pittsburgh Penguins captain Sidney Crosby tried to carry on the playoff tradition during his team's back-to-back trips to the Stanley Cup finals. He managed only some scraggly whiskers, but it was better than nothing. The Penguins won their first Cup in 16 seasons in 2009.

Chicago Blackhawks center Jonathan Toews had a chinstrap beard during his team's 2010 Cup run. That might explain why the first thing the captain did the night they won was shave. Two days later at the victory parade, not a hair could be found on his face.

During the 2015–2016 season, San Jose Sharks defenseman Brent Burns (below) and center Joe Thornton got a head start on their playoff beards, growing them out from the start of training camp. The Sharks made it to the finals for the first time in franchise history that spring before losing to the Penguins in six games.

2007

Brothers Scott and Rob Niedermayer grew matching playoff beards during the Anaheim Ducks' Stanley Cup run in 2007. The more experienced veteran, sported noticeably more gray on his chin, even though at 33 he was only a year older than Rob (above, left). But don't be fooled. Scott didn't play like an old man. With his intimidating mountain man look, the defenseman anchored the team and was named playoff MVP. The Ducks defeated the Ottawa Senators in the finals.

2008

Jaromir Jagr wore an iconic mullet early in his career. But in 2008, with the New York Rangers, the winger tried a different look: the landing strip (a thin column of hair on his chin). Jagr's facial hair made a crash landing when the Rangers lost in the second round.

2009

2010

Brothers Scott and Rob Niedermayer grew matching playoff beards during the Anaheim Ducks' Stanley Cup run in 2007. Scott (above, right), the more experienced veteran, sported noticeably more gray on his chin, even though at 33 he was only a year older than Rob (above, left). But don't be fooled. Scott didn't play like an old man. With his intimidating mountain man look, the defenseman anchored the team and was named playoff MVP. The Ducks defeated the Ottawa Senators in the finals.

2013

The 2013 world champion Boston Red Sox were not the first major leaguers to adopt playoff beards, but they came the closest to looking like a hockey team. Led by (from top) Jonny Gomes, David Ortiz, Jarrod Saltalamacchia, and Mike Napoli, the entire lineup embraced the lumberjack look.

2016

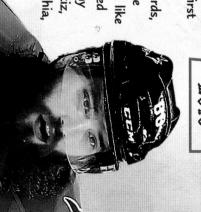

Games

Over the years there have been plenty of ways to play hockey without actually lacing up skates

▪ 1983 ▪
Bubble hockey

Dome hockey (also known as bubble hockey) was invented in 1983 by a company called Innovative Concepts in Entertainment (or ICE). Their gaming table—called Chexx—featured five skaters and one goalie per team, all controlled by handles similar to those on a Foosball table. The game action occurs under a plastic bubble to prevent the puck from flying off. The original Chexx tables featured a rematch of the classic 1980 Miracle on Ice game between the Soviet and U.S. Olympic teams.

▪ 1993 ▪
NHL '94

Still considered by many fans to be the best game in EA Sports' long-running NHL franchise, NHL '94 is an enduring cultural touchstone. Released for the Super NES, Sega CD, Genesis, and PC, this early console-style game introduced several subtle but important improvements over its predecessors, including the ability to shoot one-timers. The superstars in the game included the Chicago Blackhawks' Jeremy Roenick, Philadelphia Flyers' winger Eric Lindros, and, surprisingly, the Vancouver Canucks' Cliff Ronning, who just happened to know the founder of EA Sports since childhood.

▪ 1969 ▪
Air hockey

In the late 1960s, a group of employees from Brunswick Billiards began working on a game that would be played on a frictionless surface. By 1973, they had a patent for an "air cushion table game," in which players hit a thin puck with "disc-shaped bats." The game quickly took off and turned into a sport itself. In 1979 the first Air Hockey World Championships took place in Houston.

= 1996 =
Wayne Gretzky's 3D Hockey

Though eventually released on consoles, Wayne Gretzky's 3D Hockey first appeared in arcades as a coin-operated machine. Goofier than the NHL series of games, 3D Hockey featured hits that sent players flying and rock 'em-sock 'em fighting. The virtual goalies had the toughest time. Sometimes a slap shot would fly so fast that it set the entire net on fire when it went in. The netminders then hung their heads in shame. Other times, however, they would get their revenge, stopping the puck by literally morphing into a brick wall.

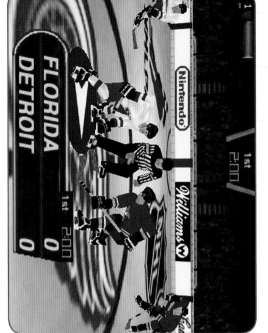

= 2002 =
NHL Hitz 2003

In a console-dominated environment, game maker Midway picked up where the arcade-style 3D Hockey left off. After the success of NFL Blitz, a football game in which players body-slammed each other after the whistle, the company released the original Hitz in 2001 and then a greatly improved sequel, which featured three-on-three game play (not counting goalies) and—true to its title—nonstop virtual bone-crushing body checks.

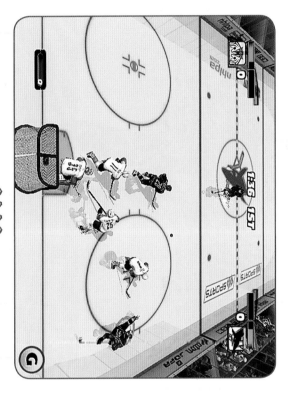

= Present =
NHL 17

With a new version released every year, the NHL franchise has come a long way since its breakout title in 1993. Regularly rated among the very best sports video games, NHL's modern versions feature all-NHL, All-Star, international, foreign league, minor league, and even major junior teams. NHL 17 also features online modes that allow gamers to connect remotely and play against their friends or strangers. A far cry from games like Hitz, the NHL games prioritize realistic graphics and simulate authentic game play.

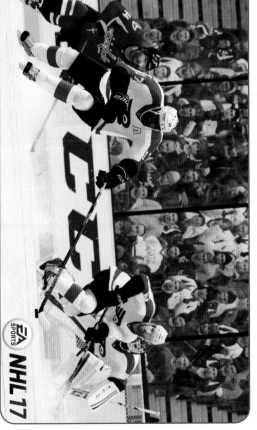

Fan Fashion

The uniforms of the players have changed, but not as much as the clothes of the NHL's faithful

THEN

Spectators didn't always wear team colors. Back in the day, as was the case for most sporting events, fan attire was very formal. Women wore dresses, and men wore suits, topcoats, and hats. Even kids were expected to dress well. This trend continued for a surprisingly long time. By the 1980s, some team T-shirts and ball caps could be found in the stands, but there were still plenty of suits. It wasn't until the 1986 playoffs, according to hockey researcher J.P. Martel, that Calgary Flames fans started a trend by wearing the team's jersey to games.

NOW

These days looking into the crowd at a hockey game can be as entertaining as the on-ice action. In 2013, a group of fans who called themselves the Traveling Jagrs, paid tribute to the well-traveled Czech star's career. Each member of the group donned a different jersey from Jaromir Jagr's 23-years-and-counting career, but all wore a long-haired wig (top left). Then there are Vancouver's Green Men, who wear head-to-toe spandex suits and taunt opposing players in the penalty box (left). From shaved heads to face paint, spectators in the stands work as hard as the players on the ice to top one another.

cards

Once thrown into one-cent packs of gum, these collectors' items now sell for thousands of dollars

FORWARD

CHI. BLACK HAWKS

Stan Mikita

HOCKEY PICTURE GUM

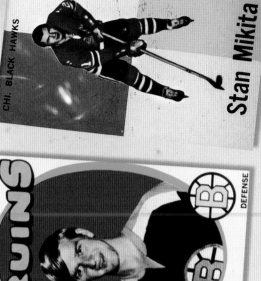

BRUINS

DEFENSE

BOBBY ORR

CANADIENS

GOALIE

KEN DRYDEN

THEN

Like the Stanley Cup, hockey cards have been around longer than the NHL itself. Starting in 1910, tobacco companies started to include cardboard photos of National Hockey Association players with their products. Collecting cards became more kid-friendly in the subsequent decade, as cards began appearing in candy and chocolate wrappers. Fans could even send in labels from household products and then receive cards back in the mail. The most famous sets, however, came in cheap packs of gum, from brands as O-Pee-Chee and Parkhurst. O-Pee-Chee and card manufacturer Topps eventually teamed up and in 1979 issued the ultravaluable Wayne Gretzky rookie card.

CENTRE BOSTON BRUINS

PHIL ESPOSITO

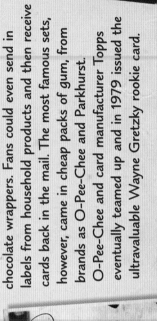

Maurice Richard

38

GEORGES VEZINA

CENTRE TORONTO MAPLE LEAFS

DAVE KEON

NOW

Hockey cards these days offer more than a picture and some stats. It's not uncommon for a modern card to feature an autograph or contain a real patch from a player's game-used jersey. Topps rival Upper Deck, which signed exclusive deals with the NHL and the NHLPA in 2004, puts out several sets for every season and even keeps the classic O-Pee-Chee line going. The company picked a good era in hockey to have a monopoly, too. Since Upper Deck became the exclusive card maker, generational talents like Capitals winger Alex Ovechkin, Penguins center Sidney Crosby, and Oilers center Connor McDavid have made their NHL debuts. The limited-edition McDavid rookie card, a part of Upper Deck's Exquisite line, regularly sells for several thousand dollars.

Over the

It's against the rules to throw stuff on the ice, but that doesn't always stop hockey's enthusiastic fans

Octopus

Detroit Red Wings fans love to throw real octopuses on the ice. The tradition started during the 1952 playoffs when brothers Pete and Jerry Cusimano hoisted one over the boards. The cephalopod's tentacles were meant to represent the eight wins the Wings needed to win the Cup. They got all eight (with no losses!) that year, and a tradition was born. The custom took on a new dimension at Joe Louis Arena. Building manager Al Sobotka was always on octopus clean-up duty. Often when he would retrieve one, he would twirl it over his head to fire up the crowd. Wings fans inspired a copycat: Before games Nashville Predators fans throw catfish.

Hat Trick

The origin of hockey's most famous celebration is unknown. The Hockey Hall of Fame website gives credit to Sammy Taft, a Toronto-based hatmaker who used to give local players a free lid after they scored three goals. Another popular story claims Taft gave his first hat to Blackhawks winger Alex Kaleta as part of a deal. Then there's the store in Montreal that claims it started the whole thing in the 1950s. Whatever the truth is, lots of headgear has hit the ice over the years. Wayne Gretzky holds the NHL record with 50 career three-or-more-goal games. That's a lot of hats!

Boards

Rat Trick

Before a game on October 8, 1995, Florida Panthers captain Scott Mellanby killed a rat in his team's dressing room with his hockey stick. When he scored two goals that night, Panthers goalie John Vanbiesbrouck dubbed the feat a rat trick: two goals and one rodent. The following spring the Panthers, in just their third season, made it all the way to the Stanley Cup finals, and fans never forgot Mellanby's feat. During the finals, the crowd at Florida's Miami Arena threw plastic rats from the stands when the Panthers scored. The following season the NHL made littering the ice a penalty for the home team.

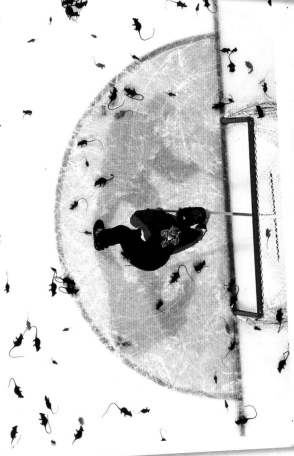

Teddy Bear Toss

While the NHL strongly discourages spectators from throwing things over the boards, some minor league and junior teams have found a charitable way to use their fans' enthusiasm for chucking stuff. Started by the Kamloops Blazers during the 1993–1994 season, Teddy Bear Toss Nights now happen all over North America. Fans are encouraged to bring stuffed animals to the rink and to throw the bears onto the ice after the home team scores its first goal. The toys are then collected and distributed to local charities. One 2015 toss in Calgary featured 28,815 flying fuzzy friends!

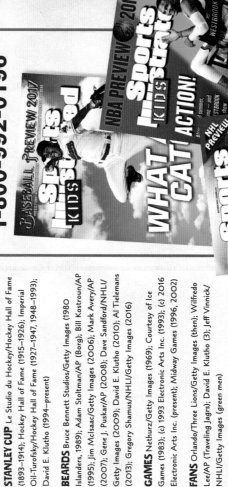
PHOTO CREDITS

COVER Transcendental Graphics/Getty Images (1930s); Pictorial Parade/Getty Images (1940s); Long Photography (1950s); Focus On Sport/Getty Images (1970s); Bruce Bennett/BBS (1980s); David E. Klutho (1990s); Gerry Thomas/NHLI/Getty Images (2000s); Claus Andersen/Getty Images (2010s)

TITLE Matthew Manor/Hockey Hall of Fame (Plante mask, Gratton mask); Tony Triolo (Cheevers mask); Portnoy/Hockey Hall of Fame (pretzel mask); B Bennett/Getty Images (Dion mask); Dave Sandford/NHLI/Getty Images (Price mask); David N. Berkwitz/Hockey Hall of Fame (sweater); Courtesy of Adidas (World Cup of Hockey jersey)

SKATES Museum of London/Heritage Images/Getty Images (bones); Ken DeMoranville/Getty Images (1800s); David N. Berkwitz/Hockey Hall of Fame (1950s, 1970s); CCM Hockey (current)

STICK AND PUCK David N. Berkwitz/Hockey Hall of Fame (1800s, 1930s, puck then); David E. Klutho (1960s, 1990s, 2000s); Michael Martin/NHLI/Getty Images (puck now)

SWEATERS Artwork Courtesy of Scott Sillcox/Heritage Sports Art (1928–1929, 1930s, 1948-49, 1962-63); Neil Leifer/Getty Images (1990s); Maddie Meyer/Getty Images (2010s)

MASKS James Rice/Hockey Hall of Fame (Benedict mask); Hockey Hall of Fame (Honma mask); Matthew Manor/Hockey Hall of Fame (1959, 1976); Tony Triolo (Cheevers); Portnoy/Hockey Hall of Fame (pretzel mask); B Bennett/Getty Images (1980s); Bruce Bennett Studios/Getty Images (1990s); Dave Sandford/NHLI/Getty Images (2010s)

GOALIE PADS David N. Berkwitz/Hockey Hall of Fame (1950s glove, 1950s pads, 1980s pads); AP (1950s blocker); Bruce Bennett Studios/Getty Images (1980s glove, 1980s blocker); Reo Roy/Brian's Custom Sports (today)

ARENAS Hy Peskin (then); Codie McLachlan/Getty Images (now); Lewis W. Hine/Buyenlarge/Getty Images (ponds); David E. Klutho (stadiums); Bob Olsen/Toronto Star/Getty Images (1931); Enzo Figueres/Moment Editorial/Getty Images (1958); Lou Capozzola/NBAE/Getty Images (1967); John Gibson/AFP/Getty Images (1983); Britta Pedersen/picture-alliance-dpa/AP (1989); Substance (2008)

PLAYMAKERS Bruce Bennett Studios/Getty Images (Cowley); Imperial Oil-Turofsky/Hockey Hall of Fame (Howe); Detroit Free Press/TNS/Getty Images (Howel); James Drake (Mikita); Denis Brodeur/NHLI/Getty Images

(Trottier); Bruce Bennett/Bruce Bennett Studios/Getty Images (Gretzky); Steve Babineau/NHLI/Getty Images (Francis, Oates); David E. Klutho (Lemieux); Don Smith/NHL/Getty Images (Thornton)

SNIPERS AP (Richard); Charles Hoff/NY Daily News/Getty Images (Howe); Bill Eppridge/The Life Picture Collection/Getty Images (Bobby Hull); Steve Babineau/NHLI/Getty Images (Esposito); Bruce Bennett Studios/Getty Images (Bossy, Burel); Jimmy Simmons/Icon Sportwire/Getty Images (Brett Hull); Patrick Smith/Getty Images (Ovechkin)

GOALIES Bruce Bennett Studios/Getty Images (Vezina, Durnan, Hall, Dryden); AP (Sawchuk); Damian Strohmeyer (Roy); Paul Sakuma/AP (Hasek); Erick W. Rasco (Brodeur)

TWO-WAY FORWARDS Bruce Bennett Studios/Getty Images (Pavelich); Focus on Sport/Getty Images (Clarke); Vincent Laforet/Allsport/Getty Images (Fedorov); Steve Babineau/NHLI/Getty Images (Bergeron)

OFFENSIVE DEFENSEMEN Tony Triolo (Orr); Andre Ringuette/NHLI/Getty Image (Karlsson)

FIGHTERS B Bennett/Getty Images (Linseman); Catherine Szenkeste/Getty Images (Roussel); Bruce Bennett Studios/Getty Images (Lindsay); Andy Devlin/NHLI/Getty Images (Luci); Melchior DiGiacomo/Getty Images (Schultz); Debora Robinson/NHLI/Getty Images (Boll)

CHARACTERS FPG/Getty Images (Shore); Bruce Bennett Studios/Getty Images (Broda, Williams); Frank Lennox/Toronto Star/Getty Images (Shack); Steve Babineau/NHLI/Getty Images (Gratton); Dick Loek/Toronto Star/Getty Images (Iafrate); Eric Miller/NHLI/Getty Images (Bergalov); Larry How/Getty Images (Burns)

PLAYER SIZE Imperial Oil-Turofsky/Hockey Hall of Fame (Worters); Steve Babineau/NHLI/Getty Images (Macavlich); Bill Wippert/NHLI/Getty Images (Gionta, Chara)

CAREERS Brantford Expositor/QMI Agency (Howe with young Gretzky); AP (Howe, with Richard); Graphic Artists/Hockey Hall of Fame (Howe, Gretzky); Scott Levy/Getty Images (Lefleur); Denis Brodeur/NHLI/Getty Images (Sakic); Bruce Kluckhohn/NHLI/Getty Image (Sakic, with Stastny); Jim McIsaac/Getty Images (Lemieux, with Crosby)

COACHES Imperial Oil-Turofsky/Hockey Hall of Fame (Adams); Le Studio Du Hockey/Hockey Hall of Fame (Day); AP (Blake, Imlach); Denis Brodeur/NHLI/Getty Images (Bowman); Bruce Bennett Studios/Getty Images (Arbur); Linda Cataffo/NY Daily News/Getty Images (Keenan); David E Klutho (Babcock); Matt Slocum/AP (Quenneville)

GLOBAL GAMES David Cannon/Getty Images (Tratiak); Per David Josek/AP (Price)

UNITS Courtesy of Slava Fetisov Personal Archive (Russian Five); Andre Ringuette/World Cup of Hockey/Getty Images (Bergeron, Crosby, Marchand, Weber); Gregory Shamus/World Cup of Hockey/Getty Images (Vlasic)

RECORDS Tony Triolo (Gretzky)

WOMEN'S HOCKEY Canada's Sports Hall of Fame-Panthéon Des Sports Canadiens (Rosenfeld); Hockey Hall of Fame (Ranscombe); Graham Bezant/Toronto Star/Getty Images (Hoffman); Brian Bahr/Getty Images (Granato); Chris O'Meara/AP (Rhéaume); Jung Yeon-Je/AFP/Getty Images (Knight); Phillip MacCallum/Getty Images (Wickenheiser)

GOALS Bruce Bennett Studios/Getty Images (Savard); David E. Klutho (Lemieux); Brian Bahr/NHLI/Getty Images (Forsberg); Paul Connors/AP (Ovechkin)

DYNASTIES Hockey Hall of Fame (Ottawa Senators); Macdonald Stewart/Hockey Hall of Fame (Toronto Maple Leafs, Montreal Canadiens); Bruce Bennett Studios/Getty Images (New York Islanders); David E. Klutho (Chicago Blackhawks)

STANLEY CUP Le Studio du Hockey/Hockey Hall of Fame (1893–1914); Hockey Hall of Fame (1915–1926); Imperial Oil-Turofsky/Hockey Hall of Fame (1927–1947, 1948–1993); David E. Klutho (1994–present)

BEARDS Bruce Bennett Studios/Getty Images (1980 Islanders, 1989); Adam Stoltman/AP (Borg); Bill Kostroun/AP (1995); Jim McIsaac/Getty Images (2006); Mark Avery/AP (2007); Gene J. Puskar/AP (2008); Dave Sandford/NHLI/Getty Images (2009); David E. Klutho (2010); Al Tielemans (2013); Gregory Shamus/NHLI/Getty Images (2016)

GAMES Nethurz/Getty Images (1969); Courtesy of Ice Games (1983); (c) 1993 Electronic Arts Inc. (1993); (c) 2016 Electronic Arts Inc. (present); Midway Games (1996, 2002)

FANS Orlando/Three Lions/Getty Images (then); Wilfredo Lee/AP (Traveling Jagrs); David E. Klutho (3); Jeff Vinnick/NHLI/Getty Images (green men)

CARDS Hockey Hall of Fame (8); Courtesy of Upper Deck (11)

THROWING STUFF Jamie Sabau/Getty Images (hats); John Biever (rats); David Reginek/NHLI/Getty Images (octopus); Rich Lam/Getty Images (teddy bears)

BACK COVER Matthew Manor/Hockey Hall of Fame (Plante mask, Gratton mask); Tony Triolo (Cheevers mask); B Bennett/Getty Images (Dion mask); Bruce Bennett Studios/Getty Images (Hayward mask); Dave Sandford/NHLI/Getty Images (Price mask)